BY JOHN BOWE

I Have Something to Say:
Mastering the Art of Public Speaking
in an Age of Disconnection

Nobodies: Modern American Slave Labor and
the Dark Side of the New Global Economy

I HAVE SOMETHING TO SAY

I HAVE SOMETHING TO SAY

Mastering the Art
of Public Speaking in an
Age of Disconnection

JOHN BOWE

RANDOM HOUSE

NEW YORK

Published in the United States by Random House, an imprint
and division of Penguin Random House LLC, New York.

RANDOM HOUSE and the HOUSE colophon are registered
trademarks of Penguin Random House LLC.

Library of Congress Cataloging-in-Publication Data

Names: Bowe, John, author.
Title: I have something to say: mastering the art of public speaking
in an age of disconnection / John Bowe.
Description: New York: Random House, [2020]
Identifiers: LCCN 2019051869 (print) | LCCN 2019051870 (ebook) |
ISBN 9781400062102 (hardcover) | ISBN 9780593133163 (ebook)
Subjects: LCSH: Bowe, John. | Journalists—United States—Biography |
Toastmasters International—Biography. | Public speaking.
Classification: LCC PN4874.B62976 A3 2020 (print) |
LCC PN4874.B62976 (ebook) | DDC 808.5/1—dc23
LC record available at lccn.loc.gov/2019051869
LC ebook record available at lccn.loc.gov/2019051870

Printed in the United States of America on acid-free paper

randomhousebooks.com

2 4 6 8 9 7 5 3 1

First Edition

Book design by Jo Anne Metsch

FOR SANTIAGO

I am larger and better than I thought.
I did not think I held so much goodness.

WALT WHITMAN

CONTENTS

AUTHOR'S NOTE

Few among us talk well or precisely about talking. The subject is too close at hand. For the sake of depicting clearly and succinctly the mechanics and moving parts of speech and the process of translating our inner selves for public consumption, I have taken the liberty, when necessary, of compressing and rearranging events and conversations. I have also, when called for, changed names, dates, and events to spare embarrassment to the many participants and family members kind enough to share their experiences and reflections with me.

I HAVE SOMETHING TO SAY

INTRODUCTION

My step-cousin Bill von Hunsdorf grew up in Dyers-ville, Iowa, an arcadian hamlet of some thousand families surrounded by a sea of corn. In eleventh grade, Bill asked a classmate to prom. She said no. Bill responded by moving to the family basement—and staying there for the next forty-three years.

He went to church now and then, but mostly he lived the life of a recluse. He taught himself to speak German. He learned to play several Chopin sonatas. He spent a decade building a model train set that wound through the entire space, gracing every bend and junction with miniature juniper trees, Old West buildings, and painstakingly detailed figures of human beings.

On the three occasions that I'd met him, Bill engaged in pleasant, if eccentric, conversation. But he remained the most socially isolated person I'd ever known. As family members reported over the years, he'd never been on a date, never kissed anyone, never held another person's hand, never shared a beer with a friend.

During the 1980s, everyone in Bill's life began to die: his father, his mother, and finally Karen, the family dog. Bill remained in the family home, year after year—alone. His shyness, long viewed as a harmless quirk, began to seem more like a life sentence of tragic solitude.

In 1992, at the age of fifty-nine, Bill surprised us all by getting married.

I learned through the family grapevine that his wife's name was Debbie, that Debbie was a nurse, that they liked to go dancing, and that they seemed very happy. What no one could fathom, of course, was how Bill had managed to talk to Debbie in the first place, much less propose to her.

In 2010, Bill and Debbie came to Minneapolis to share Thanksgiving with my family. Eager to learn how he had come out of his shell, I made sure to sit next to him at dinner. I asked him: Had he started seeing a shrink? Had he gone on meds? Nothing of the kind. As the turkey was served, Bill credited his turnaround to a nonprofit organization he'd joined called Toastmasters. Someone at church had told him it was a nice place to meet people.

The name brought to mind other clubs I'd heard of, like the Rotary, the Kiwanis, the Lions. I'd seen signs for them posted outside small towns around the country for as long as I could remember. I seemed to recall that Toastmasters had something to do with speeches, but I knew little else about it.

Bill explained he'd found a Toastmasters chapter that met weekly at the Dubuque Public Library, twenty miles from his home. He liked it from the start. The members were diverse. The fee was affordable: forty-two dollars a year. To his enormous relief, no one forced him to speak. "I didn't have to jump in until I was good and ready," he told me. "Which was all to the good, because I was, as you might say, a bit of a delicate petunia."

Toastmasters meetings typically follow a standard order. They begin with the Word of the Week, which introduces a new vocabulary word. Then there's the Joke of the Week, when volunteers stand and tell jokes. Next is Table Topics, when participants speak off the cuff about random topics. Finally, there are "prepared speeches," when members deliver four-to-ten-minute talks. At the end of the meeting, volunteer officers serving as Timer, Grammarian, Ah Counter, and Evaluator report on how long each speaker spoke, any grammatical errors they made, and the number of times they said "ah," "um," "like," and other "crutch" words, then gently offer tips for improvement.

A month after joining, Bill tried his hand at a Table Topic. He sweated, stammered, and shuddered, but resolved to try again. A few weeks later, he began to deliver prepared speeches about technical subjects near and dear to his heart, like how to install a do-it-yourself fuel efficiency monitor in your car. His fledgling efforts, he recalled with a laugh, were far from eloquent, but within a few months, he noted a tremendous improvement—both in and outside of his club.

He'd always felt anxious while talking to strangers. He'd rush his thoughts in a jumble, then become flustered when his listener didn't understand what he was saying. Through Toastmasters, he explained, he'd learned to pause before speaking to consider how his words might strike an audience. Instead of going on in his usual, dryly technical way, he began to translate his ideas into less obscure terms. Instead of presuming that his listeners would find his obsessions interesting, he began to explain *why* they were interesting. As people began to understand him better, he told me, conversations—and even relationships—became more fluid.

By now, we'd dispatched the turkey and a raft of Thanksgiving side dishes. The rest of the family had gone for a walk to make room for pumpkin pie, but Bill and I stayed behind. I was captivated by the idea that he'd transformed his life simply by delivering fewer than a dozen amateur speeches. Had learning to speak in public cured him of shyness? I asked. "Heavens no!" he laughed. "I'm still quite shy. Toastmasters did not exactly make me glib! What I learned, you might say, is a method for connecting with people *despite* my shyness—which, I will say, had a profound effect."

One Sunday, he went on to explain, two years after joining the club, Bill drove past a nice-looking woman sitting in a park by the Mississippi River. He knew that the park staged singles meets on weekends, so he pulled over, walked across the grass, sat down next to her, and delivered perhaps the most important speech of his life: "Hello. I'm Bill. I noticed you sitting here. It's such a lovely day. I wondered if you'd mind if I sit here as well."

Five months later, he and Debbie married.

I found his story profoundly moving. To a typical modern-day urbanite like me—an Internet-and-phone-addicted guy with a busy social life—organizations like Toastmasters seemed like quaint relics from a slower-paced, more congenial era. Why had I, a professed fan of things vintage and warm, never stopped to think about them? In that initial enthusiastic swoon of "discovering" Toastmasters, I imagined the club as a secret underground network of Cousin Bills, of the shyest, least heralded members of American society. In a culture dominated by loud cellphone talkers, reality TV showboats, and social media extroverts who have apparently never endured a timid moment, the existence of such an organization seemed tender beyond belief. But what I, the writer, found most appealing was that *words* had served as a kind of medicine. Bill had been sidelined, socially self-exiled. Suddenly, he had a life. He had love.

As a journalist, always on the lookout for a new idea to pitch to editors, I began to research the organization in my spare time. Toastmasters International was founded in 1924, in Santa Ana, California, by Ralph C. Smedley, a YMCA executive charged with developing adult education programs. A naturally gifted communicator himself, Smedley noted with concern the plight of students who seemed markedly afflicted by speech anxiety. Industrious, intelligent, or good-natured as they might be, their inability to communicate with ease was robbing them of normal, happy participation in personal and professional life. As he would later write, "When a man is unable to express his thoughts to his fellows, to express himself vigorously and comfortably in his business and social life, he lives a diminished existence. The greater part of his intellect, his creativity, and his very being lay dormant."

Far from quaint or out-of-date, I discovered, the organization is more popular than ever in its history, with 358,000 members in virtually every city and county of the United States and 143 countries around the world. Time and again, as I learned more about it, I was stirred by stories like my cousin's, with formerly isolated, marginalized people describing participation in Toastmasters as a life-changing, quasi-spiritual experience. "It's Alcoholics Anonymous for shy people," enthused one. Another called it the cure for the loneliness of the modern world, declaring, "It's like the opposite of depression."

I also discovered that shy rural Americans are by no means its only constituency. Chapters meet in prisons and high schools, colleges and seminaries. Hundreds of the world's most powerful corporations, from IBM to JPMorgan Chase Bank, Google, Apple, Microsoft, Coca-Cola, and Walmart host private in-house meetings. Some have more than one chapter. Bank of America has sixty-three.

As it turns out, the notion of speech education, for shy and "normal" people alike, is far from new. In the fourth century B.C., the ancient Greeks "invented" the subject as part of a larger discipline known as rhetoric. Aristotle defined it as "the ability to discover, in any particular case, the available means of persuasion."

If it seems odd to consider that such a broad subject could—or would need to—be *invented,* it helps to imagine the social realities of early democracy. Under the oligarchs who previously ruled the Greek islands with an iron fist, civic discourse was restricted to the likes of Achilles and other military heroes—and virtually forbidden to everyone else. With the advent of free speech, trials, elections, and other forums of self-rule, standing up and speaking to groups of people became, for citizens, a part of everyday life—required, in some cases, by law.

Early rhetoricians saw that certain ways of talking work better than others (telling stories in three parts, to cite an easy example). Studying, naming, and exploiting them, they realized, could transform our ability to make sense, to reach others, and to be known. The ability to influence crowds had, to a large degree, replaced military might as the primary currency of power. The study of speech became, almost over-night, the digital revolution of its day—a locus of intense intellectual activity and a turning point in the way people thought and lived their lives.

For the next two millennia, rhetoric remained a staple of education. Referred to as the "queen of the arts," it was universally understood to be *the* essential component of social, emotional, and professional success. In fact, it's hard to over-state the subject's preeminence. Western European curricula typically included years of speech training. Through the 1600s, more books were published on rhetoric than on any other subject, save Christianity.

All of which, I now realized, posed something of a mystery. The average American today speaks 16,000 to 20,000 words a day. We depend upon speech—and persuasion—as much as ever to define and explain ourselves, to give and receive orders, to make our case for love, money, and power. But the teaching of rhetoric—and public speaking—has all but disappeared. Modern education curricula train us from the age of five through our late teens and even mid-twenties to read, write, and master the processing of ideas and information *on paper*. But what about interacting live, with actual humans?

The idea of a nonprofit organization carrying the torch of an obscure, long-lost tradition emphasizing social and interpersonal skills seemed to bear upon every dour preoccupation I've ever nursed about modern life, capitalism, and technology.

In the last thirty years, the number of Americans describing themselves as "lonely" has risen fourfold. In the last fifty, the number of Americans who say they have "no one to confide in" has nearly tripled. Since the 1970s, the number of

Americans participating in public or civic groups or clubs (like Toastmasters, but also, for example, bridge clubs, political groups, religious organizations, and the PTA) has dropped by 75 percent. Recent surveys find that 65 percent of American millennials "don't feel confident" in live social interactions. Eight out of ten feel "more comfortable" texting or chatting online than conversing face-to-face.

On a societal level, the current epidemic of toxic partisanship has pundits speaking of civil war. If, as many believe, social isolation and political divisiveness are the big stories of our time, it seems worth asking: What have we lost by doing away with speech education?

For the Greeks, and for Toastmasters founder Smedley, the value of speech instruction extended far beyond mere self-improvement or vocational training. Learning to communicate well, especially with strangers, offers an antidote to alienation. As Smedley would write in his autobiography, *Personally Speaking:*

> All civilization, all progress depends on communication of ideas. . . . I believe that in bringing improvement in the way of "better thinking, better listening, better speaking" to individuals, we are contributing to the improvement of the society. Toastmasters International can be a powerful force for the improvement of world conditions. The nation needs our services, and so does the whole world.

I was moved and inspired by this spirit of practical optimism. Here was a group of people who, bucking the rage for electronic communication, deemed it worth the trouble to travel with real bodies, in real time, to meet in person and practice the bygone art of talking *face-to-face*. At first, I'd seen the club as dorky but fascinating. Now it began to seem almost avant-garde.

I wrangled an assignment from *The New York Times Magazine* to travel to Las Vegas to observe Toastmasters' World Championship of Public Speaking. Curious to learn more about the organization, I began to visit club chapters in New York, California, Wisconsin, Florida, and Louisiana. At every event and meeting, members shook my hand, looked me in the eye, handed me business cards, and said, "Feel free to ask about anything you want. Would you like to join us?" I'd never come across a group of people so friendly, warm, and polite. They were focused. They were present. No one—not once—checked their phone during a meeting.

As I toured America's Toastmasters, I met backwoods Cajuns so isolated they could barely state their names before joining the club. I watched cancer researchers with gnawed, bleeding cuticles sweat through their shirts while introducing themselves. I saw student chefs and chemical engineers with heavy foreign accents struggling to be understood but finding their voices, meeting by meeting. I interviewed former prisoners whose improved speaking skills had gotten them out of jail. I met mega-millionaires and billionaires who attributed their success—and even their happiness—to Toastmasters.

I also met frighteningly competent young professionals who seemed anything but shy. At a private Goldman Sachs Toastmasters meeting near Wall Street, I watched a group of financial analysts and software designers from around the world outdo one another with poise. When I asked one of them, a well-spoken Wharton Business School graduate, why someone so seemingly confident needed Toastmasters, she explained, "It's not just about being shy. It's about this, and she pointed from her eyes to mine and back. "It's about learning to *connect*"—the same word my cousin Bill had used.

Wherever I went, Toastmasters I met asked me which chapter I belonged to. I always replied that as a reporter (who by now had decided to write a book about the long-lost art of public speaking), my role was to remain outside the story. I loved the broad idea that speech training could serve as medicine, healing the shy, connecting the disconnected, and mending our fractious, decaying society. Public speaking seemed like a profoundly useful and positive thing for *other* people to learn.

As for me, well, like most Americans, I was terrified of public speaking.

According to the National Institutes of Health, 74 percent of Americans suffer from speech anxiety. One often hears that "Americans fear public speaking more than death."

I'd never, in forty-seven years, happily expressed myself in any kind of formal setting. Class reports, birthday toasts, interviews about my work—disaster. On the occasions when public speaking was required, I could claw my way through with a combination of bravado, hard work, a high tolerance for pain, and a sense of humor. I wasn't the worst public speaker in the world. But I never rose above the level of mediocre, and dreaded every speech I gave for days in advance.

I'd never understood why it wasn't easier. After all, I mean, in middle school, I was voted Funnest To Be With and Rowdiest Boy for three years running! In adulthood, I'd become slightly less rowdy; but still, in everyday, offstage life I was no one's idea of shy. I had plenty of friends and had traveled around the world, easily engaging with a wide variety of people. I was, in general, funny, loose, and expressive. But put me in front of a large group of people and the more I knew or cared about a subject, the worse I talked about it. After every interview or public speaking engagement, I felt a level of self-recrimination I can barely describe. *You're a phony. You're a loser.* The intensity of regret seemed indicative of a deeply psychological problem.

My inability to express myself in public had always felt like a hardwired, inexorable fact of character, an unfortunate facet of my personality installed during childhood. I'd grown up with two older siblings in a funny, verbally competitive family. As the youngest, I often found it impossible to get a word in edgewise at the dinner table. Without a doubt, the struggle—and failure—to be heard had taught me to express myself in other ways. Namely, it taught me to express myself through writing.

I attributed it as well to my upbringing in the stoic, heavily repressed culture of Scandinavian Minnesota, gently mined for decades by Garrison Keillor on his *Prairie Home Companion* radio program. Memoirist Karl Ove Knausgaard has referred to the virtual taboo against sticking out from the herd in his native Norway as "the Law of Jante"—*fit in, shut up, don't make a spectacle of yourself*—the same code I'd grown up around in the Midwest, where expressing deep belief or passion, especially in public, was shunned as pretentious.

The way I saw it, my problems with public speaking boiled down to a surplus of integrity. Whereas showier people, less principled than I, seemed to come equipped with a toggle switch allowing them to perform—and pander—like actors, I myself, incorrigibly authentic, could not so lower myself. My thoughts, I flattered myself, were simply too subtle, complicated, and even spiritual to be trotted onstage.

Before my interest in Toastmasters, I'd heard about public

speaking courses. To the extent that I knew anything about them, they seemed to revolve around the acquisition of confidence. It seemed like the province of motivational speakers, snake-oil salesmen, and nerds. If I'd thought about it, sure, it would be wonderful to be able to express my honest self. I didn't want to learn to behave in an alien, phony manner. I simply wanted to be able to express my honest self competently without feeling awful about it.

After two years of learning everything about public speaking (except how to actually do it) and another year of trying to write this book without joining the club, I finally realized that I'd been studiously avoiding the obvious. Public speaking wasn't hard for me because of my family, my hometown, my personality, or the profundity of my thoughts. It was hard because I'd never spent a moment of my life learning how to do it.

As a Toastmaster I met in Milwaukee explained (while politely laughing at me for being a coward), "Writing about public speaking without learning how to do it is kind of like a virgin writing about sex." He was right.

And so it was that, against every protesting, mortified fiber of my being, I decided to join Toastmasters and study the art of speech in the most hands-on way possible. Step by awkward step, I learned how to give a speech. As Ralph C. Smedley had promised, a painfully dormant side of my creativity, my intellect, and my very being sprang to life.

Today, with a little preparation, I can give a speech without shame, alienation, or wishing I'd said every word differently. I've gone on, in fact, to teach others to give speeches, from high school videogame designers to Silicon Valley entrepreneurs; from fashion executives and cashmere salesmen to NGO staffers who routinely address the UN; from the

CEO of one of the world's most successful charities to executives at advertising behemoth Wunderman Thompson and financial managers from BlackRock, the largest asset manager in the world.

But more important, I have learned how to connect. What does that even mean? Let me explain.

1

ACTIVE PARTICIPATION

On Wednesday, July 13, 2012, I entered the automatic double doors of Byerly's, an upscale supermarket in the Minneapolis suburb of Saint Louis Park. Beneath the over-bright lights of the gigantic overhead chandeliers, my fellow citizens hustled about, price-comparing and melon-thumping. I'd come to attend my first Toastmasters meeting, a prospect which felt only slightly more enticing than root canal surgery.

For reasons I hope to make clear over the next two-hundred-odd pages, I'd signed myself up to perform the world's most dreaded activity—in front of strangers. The decision meant subjecting myself to certain humiliation—not once but weekly, for the next six months or more.

Perhaps most daunting, I'd agreed to do so in the least comfortable environment imaginable: my hometown. Which is to say that twenty-two years after deliberately *disconnecting* from Minneapolis by moving to New York City, I'd circled back with my partner, Isabel, seven months pregnant, so she could give birth to our first child with the support of my family—while immersing myself, coincidentally, in an art form known for two millennia as *the art of connection*. I could hardly wait to explain it all to whomever I might run into from high school.

Generally, public speaking is defined as the act of delivering prepared remarks to a group of people. It's TED talks. Nobel Prize acceptance speeches. Wedding toasts and eulogies. Class reports, work presentations, and group discussions. Twenty-four hundred years ago, Aristotle, the world's greatest authority on the subject, described it a little differently. In public or private, he taught, we speak for one reason: to persuade. Speech, in his view, was a grand and ceaseless argument. In the bedroom, the boardroom, or the public square, this endless competition—my point of view against yours, ours against theirs—was actually "a partnership." It was the collective collaboration through which we develop and adjust our ideas about the foundations of civilization: justice, law, morality, and culture. To study the art of speech was more than merely learning to speak well or prettily. It meant exploring the basic operating system of human nature, the means by which we assert our identity and ultimately resolve questions of good and bad, true and false.

Isocrates, Aristotle's more successful contemporary and one of Athens's most famous speech teachers (with whom Aristotle almost never saw eye-to-eye), agreed with him on this: Speech was the quintessential human activity. For Isocrates, eloquence was intertwined with good action and larger notions of citizenship. If there was a single art form the mastery of which could make us wiser, more just, and more useful to our fellow citizens, it was public speaking.

If these ideas today seemed pie-in-the-sky, I'd interviewed hundreds of Toastmasters who seemed to prove his point. Learning to give speeches had transformed their lives and made them better, happier people.

As a writer and journalist, I'd spent much of my life studying art, music, film, literature, economics, business, design—everything I could to understand how people live and how life could be made better. But speech—as a cultural, historical, political force, much less as an art form—had never been on my radar. These ancient ideas about speech fascinated me, especially in view of the vast number of people in America and around the world who seem utterly incapable of speaking well to others. They gave me hope.

And so, despite my fear and dread, I signed myself up as my own personal guinea pig. I wanted to learn to express myself better in front of groups—to become eloquent. What would it mean, in this time of fraying social ties and decaying civic discourse, for me to learn how to connect with the people around me?

The website for Toastmasters had directed me to Club 1789, Speakeasy Toastmasters, located inside the grocery store's community room. Community rooms are locales set aside throughout the United States by libraries, nonprofit organizations, chambers of commerce, and commercial property owners for cultural and educational gatherings. As I explored the supermarket periphery, feeling my way past the craft beer shop, the in-house pet food store, and the artisanal cheese boutique, I began to worry that maybe I'd misread the directions. At last, just past the bathrooms, to the rear of the cash registers, I spied a door opening onto a classroom-looking space with folding tables, fluorescent lights, a lectern in front, and a bright gold mounted flag reading, "Speakeasy Toastmasters."

I walked in to find half a dozen friendly people milling around, chatting. By custom, Toastmasters respect new arrivals' shyness. I'd heard of people who had joined the club and sat silently for a year before finally gathering up the courage to introduce themselves. No one demanded my name or asked why I was there, but as I squeezed past a pair of forty-something women, one of them, a trim, alert-looking blonde, flagged me as a newcomer and handed me a Guest Packet.

I took a seat and pretended to peruse my brochures while observing new arrivals: A pretty, preppy Nordic woman in her thirties. A razor-stubbly man in his early forties. A tall, exhausted-looking Chinese woman in her thirties. A muscle-bound, insecure-looking guy in his twenties. A visibly stressed-out Hispanic woman in her forties wearing a cardigan and a skirt.

The officer presiding over the meeting, also known as the Toastmaster, was an exceedingly mild-mannered man in his seventies with fine, tousled silver hair. Over a yellow golf shirt, he wore a camel-colored bird-watcher vest boasting an astonishing number of pockets stuffed with booklets, guides, flash cards, Bic pens, Cross pens (matching, silver), and multi-colored markers in a neat, plastic snap-button packet. As the clock struck six, he approached the lectern.

"Good evening, fellow Toastmasters and distinguished guests," he said mildly, giving the lectern a gentle gavel-smack.

"Thank you for coming to Speakeasy Toastmasters. I'm Al Hoffman, and I'm your Toastmaster tonight. Does anyone have any questions?"

We went around the room and introduced ourselves. "Great," Hoffman continued. "Now I'll hand the floor to this week's Wordmaster, Gordon Andersen."

Andersen, to my left, was a rail-thin man in his eighties wearing a dark blue sports jacket with black suspenders and a white polyester dress shirt. His scalp shone pink through thinning hair carefully combed and oiled. As he stood, glanced around the room, and began to speak, his charisma emanated like a soothing breeze.

"Fellow Toastmasters and distinguished guests," he began, "the Word of the Week is *pursuit*. Pursuit," he repeated, "as in *hot pursuit*." He loitered an extra nanosecond on the *s* and *t,* grinning as if sharing something slightly naughty. "Or: *the pursuit of excellence. Pursuit,*" he concluded. He looked around the room, making eye contact with each and every one of us for a beat, nodded at Hoffman, and sat down, seeming pleased with himself. We clapped.

"Okay," said Hoffman from the lectern. "Now it's time for the Joke of the Week. Does anyone have any jokes?"

To my right rose a sprightly, modest-appearing woman in her seventies. From her bright-orange hair to her tiny white tennis shoes, she seemed cut from the same cloth as Andersen— elderly, Scandinavian, demure, and exquisitely self-possessed.

"Ole," she began, "is getting ready to celebrate his fiftieth anniversary."

A titter went around the room. Sven and Ole jokes are an old Minnesota standby, recounting the endless mishaps of the mythically dense Scandinavian immigrants, Sven, Ole, and

Lena (Ole's wife). As we leaned forward in our seats, she shifted into a Norwegian accent:

"Vhat are you going to do for your anniversary?" Sven says.

Ole says, "Vell, for da twentieth anniversary, I took Lena to Norvay."

Sven says, "Dat's nice, so vhat are you going to do to top dat?"

Ole says, "I tink I'll go pick her up."

The old chestnut got a laugh. Our sprightly humorist sat down, gathering our applause like a poker player raking in chips after a winning hand.

The slightly harried-looking Hispanic woman rose and stiffly recited an inoffensive riddle about cannibals; the razor-stubbly guy stood and produced an affable joke about clowns. We clapped for her. We clapped for him. As should now be obvious, the club, by design and without fail, offers the least judgmental, most forgiving environment imaginable. If a member had sobbed and wet themselves by way of telling a joke, we would have clapped for them, too.

The welcoming vibe notwithstanding, I began to succumb to a violent swoon of paranoia. *There's no fucking way I can do this.* I'd vowed before coming that from my very first meeting, I'd raise my hand and join in, despite my apprehensions. But how? None of what I was observing seemed remotely like normal human behavior. The standing up, sitting down, joke-telling, clapping, and looking around the room to make eye contact seemed entirely scripted and ritualized. *It wasn't natural.*

Desperate to subdue what felt like a rapidly impending

meltdown, I forced my eyes downward, to the *Beginner's Handbook:*

> As a Toastmaster, you'll learn to overcome the initial nervousness that everyone feels when called upon to speak before a group or audience. You will learn how to organize and present your ideas logically and convincingly. You'll improve your ability to listen to other people's ideas and evaluate them. And you'll develop self-confidence that will help you in every situation. The key to getting the most out of the Toastmaster Communication and Leadership Program is your active participation.

Here, precisely, was the problem: "active participation." If the paint-by-numbers approach to social performance seemed off-putting and even inauthentic to me, the exercises comprised Toastmasters' time-tested method of coaxing the inchoate goo of the heart and mind into lucid audible product intelligible to other humans. Whether I liked or understood them or not, they had worked out wonderfully for the four million Toastmasters who'd joined the club since its founding in 1924.

Aristotle, back in 335 B.C., described speech as a technical art, a skill that has nothing to do with personality, charisma, confidence, overcoming anxiety, or any such emotional ideas we moderns attach to the act. Like using recipes for cooking (which noncooks often view as a kind of magic), speaking in public means learning first to observe and then to master the component parts of speech.

Toastmasters, loosely modeled after the Greek approach, teaches the art of public speaking by breaking the act of communication into simple technical components: how to organize and focus your thoughts, how to use words effectively, how to use your voice and body, how to employ data and visual aids, and how to persuade and inspire an audience. By joining in, actively participating, and imitating the admittedly stiff, unnatural behavior of my clubmates, I'd learn to observe the secret workings of speech and master the art of expressing myself clearly and effectively—onstage and everywhere else. I'd seldom felt so threatened in my life.

By now I was madly overthinking and horribly self-conscious. While part of me distantly observed the tall Chinese woman telling a joke about three bakers, I tried to reassure myself by recalling the story of Roy Chenier, a former prisoner I'd met in Baton Rouge a year earlier whose Toastmasters experience I'd found inspiring.

At the age of seventeen, Chenier was arrested for robbery. He'd committed dozens of break-ins, he told me, but was, ironically, innocent of the one he'd been charged for. His public defender advised him to play it safe and plead guilty. At trial, Chenier surprised both lawyer and judge by impulsively changing his mind and pleading innocent. The judge, furious with Chenier's impudence, sentenced him to ninety-nine years in Angola State Prison.

After serving twenty-five years, he was given his first parole hearing. When the big day arrived, he was led in handcuffs to the visitors' building. With no lawyer, no social worker, no preparation whatsoever about what to say or how to say it, he was seated before a panel of five retired prosecutors, deputy wardens, and judges and left to advocate for himself.

Chenier's interlocutors peppered him with questions: "What have you learned during your incarceration? How do you think society might benefit from your release? If you're released and you can't find a job, how will you support yourself besides crime?"

He heard himself answering the parole board's questions with vague responses, like "Uh, yeah, you know, uh, you know, I ain't gonna get in trouble!" As he watched the looks of disapproval spread across his judges' faces, Chenier became more and more tongue-tied. By the end of the hearing, he found himself staring at the floor, barely able to mutter.

Chenier comes across as an easygoing guy. He told me that he had always had plenty of friends and enjoys meeting new people. Yet all his life, he said, speaking to people in authority had provoked speech anxiety. "Whenever I'd be talking to teachers or police, maybe people with a little bit of power," he explained, "I'd stop knowing how to explain myself. Even if I was tellin' the truth! And people wouldn't really believe me. Because ain't nobody going to believe you if you can't explain yourself."

Over the next eight years, Chenier was granted three more hearings. He blew them all. "Every time," he recalls, "I got denied. Denied, denied, denied."

One of Chenier's closest prison friends was a former bank robber named Ashanti Witherspoon. Witherspoon had been sentenced to seventy-five years for shooting and wounding two police officers during a holdup in Shreveport in 1972. Twenty-six years into his sentence, he joined the prison chapter of Toastmasters. In less than a year, he earned parole.

As a free man, Witherspoon became a devoted champion of prison Toastmasters programs. On alumni visits back to Angola, he urged Chenier to join. Chenier respected Witherspoon immensely, but his suggestion seemed ludicrous.

Witherspoon was a born smooth talker. Chenier was not. People like Chenier didn't learn to become poised or eloquent any more than short people learn to become tall.

Witherspoon insisted. "You need to sell yourself. Ain't nobody else gonna sell you in this world." He left Chenier with a heavy reprimand: *It is cowardly, weak, and unimaginative for a man in jail not to use every possible tool at his disposal to be free.*

Three weeks later, Chenier received some news: he'd been approved for another parole hearing. All that night, he agonized. "I needed to get out," he said. "I had to give 'em the least possible reason to say no to my freedom." He joined Toastmasters the next morning.

Chenier sat in the back of the meeting room for a month before volunteering for his first Table Topic, an exercise in which members speak extemporaneously about randomly assigned subjects. The theme: prison food. After more than three decades in jail, Chenier had plenty of thoughts on the topic. Yet, the moment he stood to speak about it, he froze. He felt the blood rush to his head. He doesn't remember what he said—only that his clubmates congratulated him afterward. He volunteered again the next week, and the week after.

His club officers encouraged him to begin working on his first prepared speech, the Icebreaker. He decided to talk about the grandmother who raised him. "She tried to steer me in the right direction," he told me. "Being young and hotheaded, I didn't want to listen. That's how I wound up the way I did."

For several weeks, Chenier mulled over his speech. At lunch, in his cell, in the prison yard, and at his job making belts for the annual Angola prison rodeo, he pondered tips from his meetings and from his instruction manual:

Memorize your introduction and conclusion so you know where to start and finish.

Break your speech into three or four parts.

Learn to rid your speech of "crutch" words like "ahh," "umm," "like," "y'know," "youknowwhatI'msayin'" and so on.

Like many novice Toastmasters, Chenier balked at the idea of altering his normal way of speaking. But as he began to eliminate "filler" words from his speech, he observed a heightened sense of clarity about what he was trying to say. As he learned to start and finish each exercise with a memorized introduction and conclusion, he noticed a distinct boost of momentum. As promised, Chenier told me, the techniques suggested by the club seemed to bolster his ability to "explain" himself.

On January 4, 2009, the guards came once again to march him to the visitors' building. He was nervous. But for the first time in his life, he had prepared himself to speak his truth. He sat down and told the parole board very plainly: "I was young and immature. I made mistakes. But I deserve another chance in life." He talked about getting his GED, about his extensive volunteer work with juvenile offenders. He explained his plan for earning a living and what he'd do if he ran into problems. As the judges asked questions, he listened. He paused, collected his thoughts, looked the panel members in the eye, and answered straightforwardly. "I showed them who I was," he said. "I told them they wouldn't regret their decision to let me be free. I meant it."

Unlike most weighty decisions in life, the results of a parole hearing are declared on the spot. Chenier's judges discussed his fate for ten minutes, then turned to him and announced: He was free. One of the judges looked particularly pleased. He smiled and told Chenier, "You did a good job talking." On March 13, 2009, after thirty-four years of incarceration, Roy Chenier walked out of Angola State Prison.

He'd been a Toastmaster for seven months.

At the lectern, Al Hoffman thanked us for our humorous contributions, then introduced the evening's Table Topicsmaster, Lynn Reed, the trim, alert blonde who'd given me my Guest Packet. Reed strode to the front of the room and, in a quick little do-si-do, switched places with Hoffman at the lectern.

"Thank you, Mr. Toastmaster, fellow Toastmasters, and distinguished guests," she said, smiling. "Tonight, our topics are organized around last week's Kenny Chesney concert at the Target Center. Do I have any volunteers?" Nearly every right hand in the room shot up. Reed chose the pretty, preppy woman in her thirties, Jen Shepard. "Jen," she said, "your topic is 'guitars.'"

Shepard rose, paused, smiled, blushed, cleared her throat, laughed nervously, glanced toward the door, brushed a hair from her face, cleared her throat again, and, at long last, began:

Um, okay.

So.

Guitars are, um, wood instruments. They have six strings.

Okay.

There are acoustic guitars. And electric guitars.

Ahh.

My brother used to play the electric guitar. He played in a band called, um, actually, the Douchebags. They weren't very popular. My parents—but I guess yeah, y'know, he had fun.

So.

Um.

I always played piano. Or at least, when I was a kid. I haven't played for a while now. But actually I'd really like to start again.

Okay. Well. Yeah. Um.

I guess that's it from me about guitars.

So. Okay.

She paused for a long beat with an agonized, fake smile. By the time we deduced that she had finished and began to clap for her, allowing her to sit, she looked altogether drained.

Reed asked again for volunteers, then called upon Bobby Marino, the muscle-bound, insecure-looking guy. "Bobby," she said, "Your topic is Tim McGraw." Marino rose, smiling sheepishly. With tight-fitting trendy clothes and a club-kid haircut, he was the youngest, least Minnesota-looking guy in the room.

"Thank you, Madam Table Topicsmaster, fellow Toast-masters, and distinguished guests," he began:

As an Italian American from Jersey City, I didn't grow up listening to a lot of country music. As a teenager, and in my twenties, I mostly listened mostly to Eminem, 50 Cent, Lil Wayne, like that. But as a matter of fact, I really like Tim McGraw. Especially that one song, "Truck Yeah." You know, it's got a pretty good melody.

One of the reasons I like him is because he's married to

Faith Hill. I always thought she was kind of hot. Another reason is because his dad was Tug McGraw, who won the World Series for Philly, which was the closest baseball team to, um, Jersey City. But it also turns out he's Italian American, too. I think his grandpa came over from Italy. So. I actually like Tim McGraw a lot.

Marino looked apprehensively from face to face for a beat before concluding, "Mr. Toastmaster, Madam Table Topics-master, distinguished guests." We clapped, and he sat down, looking relieved. His delivery, halting and tentative, was far from dazzling. But coming after Shepard's speech, his ability to proceed from start to finish without mishap seemed a significant accomplishment.

As a first-timer, I couldn't yet see how using introductions and conclusions (or not) had helped or hurt their speeches, but I'd later see how Shepard's opening tics—in lieu of an actual introduction—had gotten her off to an awkward, distracting start. Her lack of a conclusion, and the uncertainty it produced, had forced her to stare at us—and us at her—for the onstage eternity of seven seconds (I know because I recorded the whole meeting). Conversely, Marino's use of the special Toastmasters greeting had launched his speech in the swiftest, most direct way possible, making it easier for him to concentrate. His conclusion had guided our expectations like the final chord or note of a song, informing us that he had finished, letting us know we could stop listening and start clapping.

Reed turned to me, smiled brightly, and asked, "John? Would you like a Table Topic?" The entire group seemed to shift in their chairs to watch me answer. I forced my own fake smile and croaked, "Sure!"

"Good!" said Reed. "Your topic . . . is 'boots.'"

I rose, faced the group, and unconsciously reached for the part of my brain that stores greetings. I'd heard the Toastmasters salutation plenty of times, but it had never occurred to me to memorize it. Like any other form of protocol, memorized greetings and rote behavior had always seemed uncool to me. *Unnatural.*

So now. Like Shepard. I paused. Gulped. Fake-smiled again. Glanced toward the door. Thrust my hands into my pockets. And frantically began trying to speak like I do in normal life. "Uhmm," I stammered.

Ha ha!

Fellow, uh, ladies and gentlemen, I, ahhh.

After nine seconds of my groping for a way to get started, the words at last proceeded to flow. "Boots," I began, "are very important to me. In fact, they've saved my life on two separate occasions." For thirty-two seconds, my brain, voice, and body functioned in unison as I gave a surprisingly coherent account of a motorcycle accident in which my steel-toed punk rocker boots had saved my right foot from getting crushed. Thirty-three seconds in, however, I began to unravel:

The second, ahhh, such boot incident, um . . . happened . . . ahh. When I was, ummm, about thirteen. I was horseback riding. I was passing through some narrowly spaced trees. And my feet would have gotten really badly scrunched between the horse and the tree if I hadn't had boots.

So, um . . .

    I, ahhh.

    I—

My flow—my concentration, my ability to explain myself—had been disrupted by the unwelcome memory of a copse of trees, a sunny day, and my oldest friend, David Warner, circa eighth grade, laughing at me for fighting off tears as my foot, *unprotected by boots,* throbbed with pain. I'd been so flustered at the beginning of my speech, specifically thanks to the lack of a memorized introduction, that I'd chosen a story which—oops—wasn't true. So now what? I could stop my speech, admit my mistake, and spend some awkward seconds—with the clock ticking and all eyes upon me— digging up a replacement story, or I could shut up and get myself off the hot seat.

I concluded my speech as quickly as possible:

So, ahhh, if I had not had boots on both of those occasions, I ahhh, would have, ahhh, suffered from immense pain and so, ahhhh, I don't know what else to say about boots, but I think it's true to say that boots . . . are . . . y'know. In- deed . . . Ahhhh . . . Our friends. And we should always be glad for boots.

My clubmates smiled and clapped, and I sat down, con- sumed to the point of blindness with self-consciousness as they blithely moved on to the next part of the meeting. I felt like a rodeo cowboy bucked off a child-sized bull. It smarted. Shouldn't an educated adult be capable of marshaling his or her thoughts, words, voice, and body to function together in unison for one to two minutes? When I thought about the six figures I'd blown on an Ivy League master's degree, it seemed pitiful that "Boots Are Indeed Our Friends" was the best I'd managed to do.

A math teacher named T. J. Kostopoulos, wearing cargo shorts and a Hawaiian shirt, approached the lectern. "Madam Toastmaster, fellow Toastmasters, and distinguished guests," he began, "who likes to watch television?" When no hands went up, he paused and said, "Okay. Who likes to save money?" Half the room leaned forward in their chairs, offering Kostopoulos the enthusiasm he needed to continue.

His speech, he explained, would describe three different methods for getting free or inexpensive television reception. In the rote, oddly mechanical approach to social performance I found so alien, Kostopoulos described:

A) rabbit ears;
B) Hulu; and
C) some new kind of antenna that's even better than rabbit ears but the description of which went slightly over my head.

"And now," he concluded, "I've told you about three different methods you can use to get free television. Ladies and gentlemen. Fellow Toastmasters. Distinguished guests."

Everyone around me clapped, so I did, too. Kostopoulos's speech was neither informative, nor persuasive, nor funny. We clapped, of course, to be polite. But we also clapped, I realized, because he'd demonstrated his willingness to practice the weird, ritualized array of speech tricks on offer that I, as yet, could barely see.

The meeting ended. As the group broke up and other Toastmasters rose to leave, Gordon Andersen, the old gentleman seated next to me, gathered a collection of Toastmasters pamphlets into an ancient briefcase. Noticing my look of woe, he smiled kindly.

"All this stuff seems pretty incomprehensible right now, I imagine. But every nuance, every gesture, and every word that happens at a Toastmasters meeting happens for a very good reason." He gave me the mischievous look he'd worn earlier. "This club is very, very sneaky."

2

YES. YOU. CAN.

B y early August, I'd attended three Toastmasters meetings and paid a $20 membership fee and $55 for my first "semester." In exchange, I'd become Toastmasters member number 02577409 and received a lesson book called *Competent Communication*. The manual included ten exercises, each emphasizing a basic rudiment of public speaking.*

Our son, Santiago, came along in late June, healthy and thriving after a prolonged birth. Isabel, my partner, had won the lottery in terms of paid maternity leave: six months of

---

* In June 2018, Toastmasters International unveiled a new education program called Pathways, which builds on the ten-lesson Competent Communicator curriculum detailed in these pages. The new program pursues the same objectives as the traditional platform, with similar assignments and identical club, mentor, and meeting protocols, but with a greater emphasis on real-life, professional speaking contexts, an enhanced focus on evaluating and responding to feedback, and an interactive online program in lieu of the paper version. See toastmasters.org/Pathways.

full-time parenting. Our lives as happy, if sleepless, new parents had begun. I hoped to finish a speech every two weeks to complete my manual in time to celebrate the holidays with my family and return to New York after New Year's.

We'd sublet an apartment in the building where my eighty-two-year-old mother lived, an arrangement allowing for easier babysitting and shared meals. Just as happily, for the price of our cramped New York one-and-a-half-bedroom, we found ourselves commanding a three-bedroom spread overlooking beautiful Lake Calhoun.

Early one morning, eager to get started on my first speech, I sat down at our gigantic glass-topped dining room table. The instructions for the exercise, called the "Icebreaker," seemed simple enough: Introduce yourself to your group for four to six minutes by speaking about something easy, such as your family, your job, or your birthplace. Choose a topic that offers insight about your character.

A list of subjects immediately came to mind: my job as a journalist; the story of how Isabel and I met; my first experiences of fatherhood. Which one, I wondered, might best offer insight into my character? Which one would be most interesting?

Toastmasters, I'd noticed, often seemed to speak on motivational and inspirational themes like "How to Persevere in the Face of Adversity" and "The Importance of Being in the Moment." I'd always found such topics to be both corny and entirely devoid of meaning. In a world so rich with subjects, the enthusiasm for such hackneyed terrain seemed rather puzzling. The organization, I concluded, was simply a bit old-fashioned.

Hoping to inject a note of creativity into the club's aesthetic, I decided to talk about the time I got lost in the Sahara Desert with a group of Tuareg nomads and almost died. The adventure had taken place during a two-year hiatus from college spent hitchhiking around the world. Certainly, here was an experience that would offer insight into my character but, more important, would raise the bar, originality-wise, by introducing a subject no one had likely ever discussed in the history of Speakeasy Toastmasters. I fairly rubbed my hands together in anticipation.

Like most modern public speaking methodologies, Toastmasters suggests opening a speech by "grabbing" one's audience with something dramatic and vivid. You might, for example, begin with a surprising personal anecdote: "Ladies and gentlemen. Ever wake up to find yourself in the middle of a swamp, naked, with four of your rugby buddies? Uh-oh! Been there!" You can pique an audience's attention with a startling, wow-I-never-knew-that statistic: "Ladies and gentlemen, this morning, as we sit here enjoying our pastries and coffee, thirty-four hundred kiteboarders around the world will get skin cancer." You can boldly commence with a stark quotation from a famous person: "Ladies and gentlemen, in the words of Selena Gomez . . ."

Like many tips for novice public speakers, the advice makes sense—until you try it. The device (at least, in my head, as I imagined using it) felt forced and sales-y. Surely, there must be a more down-to-earth, natural way to begin a speech. After half a dozen attempts to talk into a tape recorder, telling the story the way I would in everyday life by first explaining the background, I realized that being natural wouldn't quite work; I couldn't spend several minutes introducing a four-to-six-minute speech. Somehow, I'd need to follow my manual's suggestion and launch more aggressively, conveying from the very first words the trapped, terrifying sense of being lost in the desert.

For well over an hour, I tried writing a series of introductions on my laptop, each seeking to create a you-are-here feeling:

> Fellow Toastmasters and distinguished guests: Imagine a place so barren that wherever you look, in every direction, for hundreds of miles, there are no trees, no plants, no houses, no people.

> Fellow Toastmasters and distinguished guests: Imagine a place so hot that by eight A.M. the temperature reaches 120 degrees. The air shimmers with heat waves, everywhere you look. Now imagine: You forgot to bring water.

> Fellow Toastmasters and distinguished guests: Imagine traveling beyond the edge of the map, thousands of miles from home, hundreds of miles past the nearest paved road. You have no car, no truck, no phone, no friends, no backup plan.

The words themselves were fine; I could have forced myself to say them if I'd wanted to. But there seemed to be no way to say them like I meant them while imagining an audience. *Should I lower my voice and speak more seriously? Should I brighten up and seem more lighthearted?* As I stood in front of the mirror, practicing each introduction in a dozen different ways, my hope of finding a way to say them authentically dwindled toward a kind of bafflement.

Convinced I must be overlooking something obvious, I

returned to my manual and surveyed the tips I'd found easy to grasp and incorporate: Memorize the introduction and conclusion; break the speech into three or four parts; get rid of all "crutch" words like "ahh," "umm," "y'know," and so on. So far, so good. Here were the kinds of techniques I felt I'd been promised by the club: simple, unemotional, practical, and easy to adopt. But now I noticed additional instructions: "The more personal your talk, the warmer the relationship will be between you and your audience." "Instead of thinking of this presentation as making a speech, think of it as a talk before a group of friends." The advice set me on edge. My clubmates seemed perfectly nice. But the suggestion— that I project fake warmth and *act* like we're friends—felt creepy.

For most of the twentieth century, the term "public speaking" was nearly synonymous with Dale Carnegie, author of numerous public speaking books and the best-selling self-improvement book of all time, *How to Win Friends and Influence People,* published in 1936. Carnegie's lessons boiled down to a simple precept: *The key to success is a sunny, bubbly disposition:*

> You don't feel like smiling. Then what? Two things. First, force yourself to smile. If you are alone, force yourself to whistle or hum a tune or sing. Act as if you were already happy, and that will tend to make you happy.

Exhorting students with inspirational commands like "Go in There and Fight" and "Wham It Across," Carnegie taught public speaking with the subtlety of a klaxon. The more confident and pleasant you can be in a presentation, the greater the chances that people will believe and like you. Be loud! Be big! Be brash! Be confident! "If it works in the movies," he coached, "it will work in real life!"

Carnegie's teachings had helped millions of people muster the courage to speak in public, but for modern sensibilities, or at least for mine, his methods seem antiquated and, worse, insincere.

But from the "invention" of rhetoric (the ability to discover, in any particular case, the available means of persuasion) in the fourth century B.C., the Greeks seemed to grasp that the study of speech as an art form implies an acceptance that such notions—of sincerity, authenticity, and even truth and falsity—are more complicated than we like to believe. Nice as it is to imagine that speech and our very identity flow from our souls like a virgin stream from a natural spring, a survey of our behavior on any given day hints at a degree of underlying creativity and flexibility about who we are and who we wish to be: we speak with different selves to children, spouses, friends, enemies, subordinates, and superiors. Are we, in such moments, deviating from a fixed, authentic self? Or is speech—and the performance of our selves—composed of a constant weighing of choices? With no pejorative connotation whatsoever, the Greek word for "oratory," like the word for "acting," is derived from the verb "to sift" or "to interpret." Here, at heart, was the discipline of rhetoric: How do we use our voice, body, and words to get our point across?

As early philosophers and teachers of rhetoric delved into this new, objective approach to language and communication, they began to identify and name the parts and functions of speech, homing in on their particularly persuasive capacities. One early rhetorician specialized in teaching the benefits of framing legal arguments in the most advantageous manner possible. Another wrote treatises extolling the power of using certain vocal tones, hypnotic rhythmic and poetic devices. Subsequent professors of rhetoric gained fame with treatises exploring the latent power unleashed through clever use of introductions, conclusions, metaphors, and epithets, even verb tenses—all in service of exploiting every obtainable gain in expressiveness and persuasive power.

If it sounds absurd and obscure, take the example of verb tense, which, most likely, you've never thought about at length. If you want to blame someone and keep them in the doghouse, keep the conversation in the past ("You haven't taken out the garbage for three months"). If you want to escape blame, don't wallow in the past ("That's not true! I took it out, um, five Wednesdays ago, on the eighteenth of last month!"); shift the conversation toward the future ("You're right, I'm going to do better from now on"). Like most people, you've probably used this stratagem unconsciously in everyday conversation. Now try using it consciously. Here's where the power of rhetoric becomes clear.

In the hands of scrupulous teachers, such rhetorical devices proved useful teaching exercises for training the newly minted citizens of ancient Greece to assert and explain themselves, to defend their views and opinions ably enough to participate in the elections, trials, and public debate forums of early democracy. But in a historical, political moment where the ability to sway the masses had become the newest, surest means to power, it's easy to see how for the less ethically inclined, the abuse of such newly "weaponized" communication techniques proved irresistible.

As the political process of the day became increasingly dominated by the nascent equivalent of lawyers, politicians, campaign strategists, and the like (collectively known as *rhetors,* or professional public speakers), public discourse became something like an arms race for winning at any cost, truth be damned. To compare the effect to modern politics—which is of course my naked, sole intention—imagine, if you will, the most shameless negative campaign styles, in which politicians and their surrogates abandon all pretense of substance to traffic in fake news, haranguing one another for slips of the tongue and making outlandish accusations. *Politician X wants to impose the death tax! Politician Y is a Communist cocaine addict!*

As could easily be predicted, public debate, unmoored from ethical parameters, became increasingly vitriolic and demagogic, paralyzed by partisan gridlock, and incapable of solving the problems of the day. To cautious, sober, intelligent observers, the inescapable conclusion seemed to be that the black art of rhetoric had led Greece into the gutter. Plato, among others, would fulminate for years, writing pamphlets questioning the value and morality of its teaching. How could an art form so tailor-made for facilitating deceit prove beneficial to humankind? The question—is rhetoric good or bad?—has dogged the subject ever since.

In approximately 335 B.C., Plato's former student, Aristotle, would publish a series of lecture notes known as the *Ars Rhetorica,* precisely in answer to the question. We learn rhetoric, wrote Aristotle, not in order to lie better, but because learning to see arguments from all sides and learning to see the constituent components of persuasion aid us in disarming those who would manipulate the masses. Implicitly the text is a kind of user's manual for citizens of a democratic political system: In a world of liars, rogues, and people with naturally differing opinions, good people—people like you, reader—

can't just sit there whining because others argue vulgarly and unfairly. Democracy requires your participation.

If his predecessors had explored rhetoric in piecemeal fashion, one trick at a time, Aristotle, aptly described by writer Sam Leith as "the Newton of rhetoric," delved more deeply, comprehensively, and systematically into its workings, conceiving of the discipline as "essentially a theory of human nature." We agree with speakers less because they are right or because their facts are unassailably correct than because we find them credible. We listen to speakers and find them appealing because we feel they are speaking to our interests, with our happiness in mind. These psychological notions—of credibility and happiness—would prove the bedrock of everything one ever need learn about public speaking.

Returning, then, to the question at hand of how we use our voice, body, and words to get our point across, the answer, for Aristotle, was simple: When you're thinking of how to speak, first and foremost, think about how people listen. "The audience," he would write, "is the end and object of all public speaking."

The words initially struck me as a nicely phrased observation: The public is an important part of public speaking. But as I would learn only over the course of several more speeches, Aristotle's simple phrase—no observation, but rather a command—would supply the technique for overcoming speech anxiety and everything else I'd ever need to know about public speaking.

Inspiring as I found them, Aristotle and the ancient Greeks had helped me in no way whatsoever to plow through my speaker's block. In the end, I'd unhappily settled for one of my you-are-there introductions. My desert story continued to feel entirely alien. As I drove to the meeting, took my seat, waited for the prepared speeches portion of the meeting, and proceeded, numb as a post, to deliver it, I felt as panic-stricken as I'd ever felt before any formal presentation in my life.

Speakers often use phrases like "I had them" or "I lost them" to describe their success or failure at "connecting" with an audience. The terminology only figuratively articulates the ambition of the would-be orator, but in the act of failure, its meaning becomes easier to grasp.

By mumbling at times instead of speaking clearly, I rendered, say, 10 percent of my words incomprehensible—hard for my audience to connect to. By slouching, cowering, and grimacing—calling attention to my discomfort instead of my story—I diminished our connection still more. By dropping in words and phrases in basic French, ignoring the fact that my audience likely didn't speak French (never mind that I was self-deprecatingly trying to reenact my own ignorance of French at the time of the story), I chipped away still further at any sense of connection. By blithely omitting *any* explanation for why I'd taken such a dangerous journey in the first place (didn't everyone in their twenties have a death wish?), I made it hard for them to relate to the story—and to me.

As I squandered the invisible rhetorical tethers that connect a speaker to an audience, all I could sense of my speech going awry was how it played across the faces of my fellow Toastmasters: Gordon Andersen, gently biting his lip; Margo Forster's eyebrows shooting up; and the stressed, fraught expression on the face of a tattooed young hipster woman who visited twice, then never returned.

At the end of the meeting, Jen Shepard, the woman from

the week before who'd used no introduction or conclusion, stood to deliver my evaluation. Toastmasters typically offer what's called the Oreo Cookie approach to criticism: praise, constructive criticism, praise. Shepard lauded me for my humor; for memorizing my speech; for maintaining good eye contact; and for not clinging to my notes, as many first-time speakers do. After noting that I'd mumbled, shoved my hands into my pockets, and balled them into visible fists, she advanced to her biggest complaint. "The desert thing was really interesting," she mused, "but it seemed kind of 'out there' in terms of relatability." Concluding with an affectionate nose-crinkle, she said, "Not bad for a first crack. I thought you were very endearing."

I doubt that I performed significantly better or worse than the average first-timer. I'd expected my maiden effort to be embarrassing, and—no surprise—it was. After the meeting, however, as I drove to meet Isabel and Santi for dinner, I plunged into a state several shades darker than mere embarrassment.

Reviewing my previous mishaps with public speaking, I realized that the sting of fiasco wasn't in making an ass out of myself or coming across as an imperfect person so much as failing to communicate the depth, thoughtfulness, engagement, and concern that I know myself to possess. Speaking poorly in public was a waste of the audience's time, and a missed opportunity to share something of value. I'd dedicated my life as a writer to the express purpose of creating meaning, at least on the page; how absurd, how profoundly distressing, then, to be unable to do so in person—with my real self.

Somewhere in the unexamined backwaters of my mind, I'd cherished the idea that my public inexpressiveness had been a choice, a kind of coyness, and that if the day came when I *really* felt like it, the mere decision to open up would unleash, if not torrents, then at least a reasonable degree of eloquence. I'd saved up—no, curated—tens of thousands of thoughts, memories, and observations. Surely, at least in theory, there must be some meaningful, helpful, brilliant, or even semi-brilliant way for them to come tumbling out. What, otherwise, would be the point of my many years of thinking, observing, reflecting? My Icebreaker speech marked the first time in my life that I'd left nothing in reserve, trying as fully as possible to be clear, sincere, and direct. No padding. No detours. No irony. But I'd unleashed absolutely nothing and represented myself, if anything, even less accurately than I had in the past. It felt terrifying. *What if I just can't do this?*

Isabel and I met at a sports bar named Bunny's. As I looked around the boisterous saloon (Twins against the Red Sox on several big screens), my eye fell enviously upon the happy-go-lucky diners and drinkers, socializing with seeming nonchalance. Why is talking so easy when we're not trying to do it well? I felt supremely disheartened. Where normally I would have brightened at the sight of Isabel in her purple summer dress, casual and carefree in the long weekend of postpartum sabbatical, and Santi, asleep in her lap wearing an absurd beanie with antlers, my reaction was muted by self-pity. Isabel looked up from her menu and clocked my mood immediately.

"Wanna talk about it?"

Reverting to couple's shorthand, I answered, "Failure."

"In terms of . . . ?"

"System-wide."

In the halting, clunky, three-to-five-syllables-at-a-time manner I adopt when I'm upset, I began to choke out an explanation. "It just felt like . . . these different facets . . . of whatever . . . personality . . . devices . . . trying to coordinate them . . ." I faltered, unable to finish the thought.

For several years, we'd been noting my habit of periodically fading out like this, midsentence. Referring to the spinning Mac cursor that appears during moments of computational paralysis, Isabel and I called it "the spinning rainbow wheel of death." (Apparently, we're not the first to land upon the term.) It usually happened in the middle of a fight or an otherwise fraught discussion. At the moment of spitting out the last few words of a thought, ostensibly something important, I'd *catch*. I could never diagnose whether I was too scared to say what I meant, or if I ultimately wasn't convinced what I was saying was accurate enough to sign off on. Whatever the case, at the very moment of self-revelation, I'd taper off and lose my courage. Or clarity. Or something.

The habit understandably frustrated Isabel, who simply wanted to understand me and keep the conversation moving along. Her bearing in such moments would shift ever so slightly as she waited, expectantly, head jutted forward and eyes narrowing, a transformation of mien I invariably—and incorrectly—interpreted as impatience and criticism. I'd fairly howl to myself in response: *How could she be so unreasonable?* Never mind that I was misinterpreting her look. We'd find ourselves squaring off—me hissing at her to mellow out, she hissing at me to stop hissing at her. We'd soon be dissecting our communication problems instead of resolving whatever we'd started talking about.

Kindly ignoring the issue for the moment to stick with the topic, Isabel asked instead, "Okay. Did you forget what you were supposed to say?"

I shook my head.

"Did you become catatonic and stare at the ground or otherwise fail to be human?"

"No, I just sucked. My evaluator said it was 'a little out there' in terms of relatability."

Isabel's face softened with slight recognition. She sat back in her chair. "Well, I've heard the desert story a few times, and it's definitely pretty wild. I can see how someone just meeting you might find it hard to get their head around."

The waiter came—friendly, nose ring, dyed hair—and began reciting specials. I found myself fuming. I'd joined Toastmasters with the lofty goal of learning to become eloquent. Now, it seemed, the club and my partner had joined forces to circumscribe my efforts by telling me which topics were off-limits. "Why would it be wrong to talk about the Sahara Desert?" I asked.

So here, at this point, let's freeze-frame. Aristotle, who is, after all, Aristotle, had written that public speaking begins and ends with the audience. I, who am not Aristotle, was insisting, "No! I get to think first of myself and talk about whatever I find interesting, even if other people don't get it."

Isabel, recognizing my stubbornness, paused, smiled wanly, and deadpanned, "Well, maybe you should just quit?" At the moment, it seemed sorely tempting.

The next morning, during a furious downpour, I picked up the phone and called Susan Cain, author of the best-selling book *Quiet: The Power of Introverts in a World That Can't Stop Talking*. I'd messaged her through her website and explained my book's mission, and she'd kindly agreed to an interview. Cain's book would eventually spend years on the *New York Times* best-seller list, fulfilling her childhood dream to be a

writer, but in turn creating a problem. Cain, a lifelong intro-
vert, was now required to speak to large audiences . . . about
her aversion to speaking to large audiences. She'd once been
so nervous about a law school presentation that she'd vomited
on her way to class.

I was eager to chat with Cain for several reasons. For start-
ers, everything I'd read about rhetoric and its history had
concerned men. The first woman's entry in virtually every
compendium of "great American speeches" is Susan B. Anthony's 1873 speech about women's suffrage. On a personal
level, I was eager to talk to Cain because I'd identified with
what I'd read about her struggles to master public speaking.

When Cain first hit the speakers' circuit, she'd complained
to friends about how emotionally wrenching it was. Their
response—that she look into speech training—provoked resistance. "There's this idea," she said, "that to speak well in
public, you have to be really peppy and revved up and be this
rah-rah showman running around onstage, keeping everybody in stitches. I just don't think that's how most people
really want to be." Speech training seemed patently inauthentic, she said. "It just seemed like learning these artificial, theatrical techniques, like how to amplify your voice and how to
use the right vocal inflections."

One day, one of Cain's friends asked if her antipathy to
artifice wasn't a bit naïve. After all, we wear clothes instead of
walking around naked. We brush our teeth instead of spew-
ing bad breath. We cook our food, adding spices and oils. A
thousand times a day, we alter ourselves and the raw materials
around us, not to deceive, but to improve the quality of our
experiences. Had Cain written her book at a single sitting, as
a first draft, feverishly dashed off like a diary entry? Or had
she rewritten it many times, clarifying and compressing her

ideas to improve her readers' experience? Maybe, her friend suggested, artifice in speech could be viewed as a way to enhance one's truth, rather than obfuscate or cheapen it.

In early 2011, Cain relented and enrolled in a workshop at the Public Speaking Center of New York. Soon after, she joined a Toastmasters chapter in a suburb of New York City. Just one year later, in February 2012, she delivered a TED talk on her subject—the struggle faced by introverts in a world that unquestioningly valorizes extroversion. With thirty-five million views and counting, it's one of the most popular talks in TED history.

Cain begins the speech gripping a schoolgirl's leather duffel bag in both hands while recounting her first trip to summer camp. She'd packed ample reading material, assuming that camp, like home, would be a nice place to spend time with others in rich, intimate, thoughtful silence.

"I had a vision of ten girls sitting in a cabin, cozily reading books in their matching nightgowns," she explained with a smirk. As she discovered, however, "camp was more like a keg party without any alcohol."

Setting down her bag, she says:

On the very first day, our counselor gathered us all together. And she taught us a cheer that she said we'd be doing every day for the rest of the summer to instill camp spirit. And it went like this:

R—

O—

W—

D—

I—

E!

> That's the way we spell "Rowdy!"
> Rowdy! Rowdy!
> Let's get rowdy!

Cain impersonates the counselor, ironically performing a kind of cheerleader–pep rally dance, finishing with "jazz hands" and a showy Broadway gasp.

By now, the audience is laughing, and so is Cain, who continues:

> I couldn't figure out for the life of me why we were sup-
> posed to be so rowdy. Or why we had to spell this word
> incorrectly. But I recited the cheer. And I just waited for
> the time when I could go off and read my books.

Cain's book analyzes the obstacles faced by introverts and the admittedly imperfect strategies she discovered for overcoming them. "We can stretch our personalities," she writes, "but only up to a point." Judging by her speech, it seemed that Cain had stretched herself to a remarkable degree—from vomit to thirty-five million views.

I was desperate to learn how someone as sophisticated and sensitive as Cain had broken through her inhibitions and survived the mortifications of her initial Toastmasters speeches. What technique had she found to overcome her initial inhibitions?

Cain told me that in order to "really connect," you need to prioritize your audience. "It's hard if you're suffering under the cognitive and emotional load of anxiety," she explained, but there are techniques for cutting through the fear, like "envisioning" the audience and the venue before giving a speech, and "speaking from the heart." I'd heard these tips before. Most of them can be found on any of the dozens of websites devoted to public speaking. I'd read them, stared at them, mused about them at great length. They hadn't helped. I began to worry: Maybe I was so alienated, so unique, or so weird that my strain of speech anxiety was fundamentally different than other people's. We went in circles for a few more minutes, me talking about the agonies of my paralysis and she tactfully bringing us back to the *audience.*

At last, she said that she had to go (as it happened, to prepare for a speech). Gently, she concluded, "Your ideas of what it means to learn the techniques and principles and so on are wrong." What did she mean? I hadn't the foggiest idea. But it was hard to dismiss her counsel, given her wonderful speech and—again—her thirty-five million views. As we hung up, I felt just like I had in the Sahara Desert, watching the last possible rescue vehicle passing, then receding into the distance.

One week later, I pulled into the Byerly's lot for my next Speakeasy meeting. By now it was late July. The cathedral beams of early-evening sunlight seemed to slant with a passing-of-summer quality I remembered from childhood. Like an old melody, it triggered a rush through time, to childhood and back to the present. How had I gone from Funnest To Be With boy to an adult whose idea of a good or at least meaningful time was to trudge weekly into a classroom for the purpose of retrieving the ancient "art of connection" for the, um, salvation of modern American public discourse? It seemed ludicrous. *Why not just stay in the car and enjoy the sunlight?*

Resisting nature's siren call, I rolled up the windows, exited the car, and nearly stepped into the path of Lynn Reed, the woman who'd presided over Table Topics at my first meeting.

Reed, I'd learned, worked for a prominent national bank, leading a technical sales team. Like a lot of Toastmasters I'd met, she'd entered the workforce as an engineer, then proven herself so capable that she'd been promoted into management, where, unexpectedly, her lack of people skills proved a stumbling block. Her current position often landed her onstage to lead product demonstrations before hundreds of subordinates, a task she'd never relished. Like me, she'd never aspired to be a talker, an explainer, the kind of person who charmingly, articulately chatters away onstage. But as her boss had made all too clear, her job depended on it.

Reed had arrived with her husband, Gary Milter, a software salesman with almost platinum blond hair of a type you rarely see outside of Scandinavia, who'd just returned from a lengthy business trip. Gregarious and laid-back (he'd played bass for many years in a Springsteen cover band), he seemed like the perfect counterpart to his more buttoned-down wife.

"Hey, man," he said, shaking my hand, bro-style, "We're gonna get some Vita Coco. Wanna come with?" As we strode through the aisles, passing the produce and coffee products, Milter asked, "How'd your Icebreaker go, John?" I nearly choked. It hardly seemed the time to vent my ruminations about the decline of civic discourse in America, nor my personal fears of voicelessness, so I shrugged and mumbled something like "Ahhh–it–was–ah–well."

Milter seemed to understand. "Hard to make that connection, right?" His wife leaned in and beamed with sympathy. There it was again, the word everyone seemed to use to describe the magic of public speaking. I'd love to say the cou-

ple looked cult-y or robotic, but they looked perfectly lucid
and kind.

Pleasant as the run-in had been, my positive feelings about
Milter nearly vaporized just an hour later. We'd arrived at the
prepared speeches portion of the meeting, where, as chance
would have it, he was delivering his tenth and final speech
from the manual, an inspirational exercise he had appropriately titled "To Inspire."

After greeting us and flashing a bright smile, he began:
"There are three words that I want you to take away tonight:
Yes. You. Can." The speech consisted of three stories depicting everyday people overcoming extreme difficulties—
a physically disabled marathoner, an athlete with a dying
mother, an infant possessed by a staggering will to live. At the
end of each account, Milter paused dramatically, spread his
arms apart, opened his palms, and in sheer awe of his heroes'
determination asked, "Are you kidding?" He explained what
each story meant to him personally, suggested how we might
apply this meaning to our own lives, then looped back to his
inspirational payload:

Yes. You. Can.

Each time he circled back to the "Are you kidding?" and
the "Yes. You. Can." and the choreographed gestures, I felt
myself deflating. Why had Milter abandoned the likable, free-
spirited "Born to Run"–playing lover of coconut water for
the wooden persona of a Tony-Robbins-in-training? And
why did no one at Toastmasters seem to care as much as I did
about being genuine, about being themselves, about being
original?

I'd noticed at my first meeting the pleasure Gordon Andersen took (and gave) when he spoke. From the start, he'd been my favorite. As we left the meeting that night, following Milter's speech, I walked with Andersen and crossed the parking lot toward his car. I asked him—carefully—why Toastmasters never seemed to talk more about their personal lives, their thoughts about current events, global warming, the rise of China as a superpower, or anything else they might have felt strongly about.

Andersen looked amused by my question, then peered over his glasses at me as if remonstrating with a five-year-old. "We're not here to entertain you! We're here to study how people communicate!" Elaborating on the premise that self-expression is reducible to technique, he explained, "There are parts to speeches. Every kind of speech you can find. Introduction, main body, argument, transition, conclusion. It's all technique—easily defined, readily observed. But you can't see it if you're distracted by the subject. So politics, personal stuff, controversial subjects—Toastmasters steer clear of that. We're here to practice classical speech technique, not to get people agreeing or disagreeing with what we're saying. You get me?"

Early the next morning, before Isabel and Santi awoke, I began working on my second exercise, "Organize Your Speech." In their simplest form, my manual explained, most speeches proceed from an introduction to a main body, then end with a conclusion.

The most substantive section of a speech, the body, is typically composed of three to five main ideas, points, examples, case studies, and so on. For the sake of clarity and momentum, these ideas or parts must be organized around a larger conceptual structure. A *chronological* structure deploys a topic in sections along a timeline, from beginning to middle to end. A *spatial* plan arranges a topic in different places or geographical directions. A *problem-solution* framework defines and presents an issue, explains the harm it causes, then articulates a proposed solution. A *compare-and-contrast* rubric allows the side-by-side analysis of a matter of concern. In addition to being clear with my structure, my manual said, I should make sure my choice of topic was clear, timely, and relevant for my audience. I should strive to be clear with all transitions between one part and the next, letting my audience know at all times where I am as I progress through my organizational scheme.

Eager to avoid choosing a topic that would prove too "out there," I decided to speak about a subject my clubmates might easily identify with: my hatred of public speaking. I hoped they would find it funny and relatable at the same time. If so, my story—about one of my worst public speaking mishaps— might loosen things up while speaking to feelings they'd perhaps shared.

Fifteen years earlier, I'd been invited to appear on a popular NPR show in New York City to discuss a book I'd co-edited. The book was an oral history of work in America, with interviews with hundreds of Americans—from supermodels and CEOs to farmworkers, homicide detectives, doctors, line cooks, factory workers, even a crime scene cleaner—talking about their lives and their work. A week before going on the show, nervous about screwing up, I'd asked a friend with lots of media experience for advice about how to handle it. "Just be yourself," he laughed. "Avoid getting into ridiculous amounts of details. Watch your swearing. Be likable. That's it." Off to the studio I went.

After an easygoing discussion about the colorful personalities I'd encountered and what they'd taught me about working life in twenty-first-century America, the host of the show said, "Cool! Let's talk about you, John! What about *your* experiences with work?" Unprepared for the question, I tried to deflect it by countering, "I think the people in the book are actually way more interesting than me!" The host insisted. "Oh, I'm sure you've got some stories! Tell us, what's the least favorite job you've ever had?" Sincerely, but without considering what my answer might sound like, I stuttered, "Um. Well, I guess *this*. Y'know? Being interviewed. 'Cuz I just. Like. Yeah." I'd aimed for self-deprecating, but somehow fumbled; my comment had landed as an insult. My host looked shocked and even a little hurt. In thirty seconds the interview was over and I was shooed out the door.

On my way down in the elevator, I wondered how my attempt at candor had come across as hubris. Maybe going on someone's radio show and telling him you hate being there wasn't a great strategy. When I replayed the mishap to my adviser friend, protesting that he'd told me to be myself, he paused, aghast at my cluelessness. "Well, I didn't think you'd be *that* self." The anecdote, for me, typified the problem of public speaking. Why can't you just be yourself when you speak to a crowd?

Now, eager to delay wrestling once again with my speech anxiety, I'd fled our apartment to work at the St. Louis Park public library. What I needed, I decided, was to become more familiar with great speeches throughout history. How do real speakers begin and organize their texts? What does a great speech even look like? I found the text of a 1955 address by Martin Luther King, Jr., delivered at the Holt Street Baptist Church in Montgomery, Alabama, a speech later called the spark that ignited the civil rights movement. I found the transcript of President Ronald Reagan's 1987 Brandenburg Gate speech, frequently described as a catalyst of the collapse of Communism and the Soviet bloc. I read the 1873 speech mentioned earlier, by Susan B. Anthony, the pioneer of women's suffrage, questioning why, five years after passage of the Fifteenth Amendment, women were still denied the right to vote. Finally, I watched a video of a radio chat, later dubbed "The Bacon, Beans, and Limousines Speech," by the cowboy humorist Will Rogers, one of the most beloved entertainers in U.S. history, addressing the nation at the height of the Great Depression and discussing the need for wealth redistribution.

The speeches proved revelatory, moving, fluid, powerful, and brimming with passion even in printed form. None of them, however, seemed to follow the format suggested by Toastmasters. I understood why I should choose a topic that wasn't too "out there" for my group. But did I really have to follow the cookie-cutter organizational template suggested for newcomers? My manual seemed to suggest that at the end of each section, I should tell my audience, "Okay, I've finished that section, now I'm moving on to the next one!" I could see why someone with less storytelling experience might need to follow the advice, but for a seasoned writer, it seemed like training wheels. My NPR story already had a clear beginning, middle, and end. Why bloat the narrative with unnecessary information?

For days before my meeting, I practiced my speech. I recited it in front of Santi, now eight weeks old, cooing away in his porta crib. I stood in front of the mirror, rehearsing aloud when Isabel wasn't around to watch. Before long, I'd memorized my speech well enough to throw away my notes.

From time to time as I worked, I checked my manual to confirm I wasn't forgetting anything. Was my speech timely? Well, it wasn't untimely. Was it relevant? Yep. Had I organized it? Absolutely. Had I made my transitions clear? Well, no, but unlike typical neophytes, *I* didn't need to. So, voilà. The goal of the exercise was to organize my speech clearly, and in my own way, I'd done exactly that. Except for feeling hollow, false, and riven with a sense of impending doom, it seemed to me I was doing a terrific job.

When Wednesday came and my turn came up, I took the lectern. "Madam Toastmaster, fellow Toastmasters, and distinguished guests," I began:

> Tonight, I'd like to tell a story that shows just how bad I am at public speaking. But it also shows why, I believe, people—people who aren't, say, game show hosts—hate it so much. It's a story about trying to be myself, and finding out that that's the last person you should be while talking to an audience. The question I'd like to ask is this: Is it possible to truly be yourself while facing a group of people?

I'd felt certain that choosing a subject more aligned with my audience's interests would make it easier to connect. Indeed, as I introduced my topic, making healthy eye contact and moving about freely from behind the lectern, my clubmates' eyes seemed bright with recognition. I *had* them. By the time I'd elicited a sprinkling of titters, I felt sure of it. Two minutes into the speech, however, their interest seemed to dull. Bobby Marino, the club kid, looked disengaged and blank-eyed. Alex Čapek, the razor-stubbly guy (who, I'd learned, worked as a salesman for a national beverage company), seemed preoccupied. Anne Schiffer, an advertising executive in her forties, looked on with an absent, faraway grin. As I prattled away, imitating a practiced raconteur, complaining about the stress of talking about myself (while talking about myself and pretending not to be stressed), I felt my hold—on my words, my subject, the audience, and my body—become lighter and lighter. When I finished and took my seat, I felt flushed with the same marrow-deep embarrassment I'd suffered every other time I'd spoken in public.

At the end of the meeting, Bobby Marino rose to deliver my evaluation. He praised my choice of topic, my eye contact, and my humor, but noted I needed to take better command of my diction. "You have a way of eating the ends of your sentences," he said. In terms of body language, he advised, I should take my hands out of my pockets and stop balling them up into fists. His main criticism, however, pertained to my transitions. "You really have to tell us when you're moving from each part of the speech to the next," he explained. "You know, that whole thing of tell 'em what you're gonna tell 'em, tell 'em, then tell 'em that you told 'em. You gotta make it more obvious. Cause that's, like, the kind of goal here."

I'd found the evaluation frustrating. Marino was reciting from an inspirational, motivational playbook that might have made sense within the bubble of Toastmasters, but it wasn't really the gestalt I was after. Couldn't he see that I was trying to do something more cutting-edge than what he was used to? I walked out of the meeting in a bad mood, and once again I found myself trudging beside Gordon Andersen.

When I asked him what he thought, Andersen offered, "Your story was okay, but it seemed like something you'd tell at a bar instead of to a group of Toastmasters." Reminding me that Toastmasters gather expressly to observe, study, and prac-

tice classical speech technique, he pointed out that by ignoring the core requirement of the exercise, I'd telegraphed to
my fellow Toastmasters that I wasn't interested in them. "If
an audience doesn't feel like you're speaking their language,
or talking specifically to them," he said, "you're just kind of
babbling."

He referred me to a supplemental online Toastmasters
manual called *Selecting Your Topic* and suggested I give it a
browse.

"Before you speak," the manual advised, "research your
audience. . . . Match the content and direction of your speech
to the needs of those who will be attending." Continuing, it
suggested asking myself some questions before choosing a
topic:

How many people will attend the speech?

Who are they?

What's their age range?

How familiar are they with you or your subject?

Does your audience have similar education, interests,
    backgrounds, and experiences?

What's the occasion for the speech?

Is there a theme?

Why have you been chosen to speak?

The manual made clear that I should ask these questions
before choosing a topic, *before* writing or delivering my speech,
that I should think about my audience as a group of real
people and not, say, as a scary, amorphous abstraction. As
simple and obvious as it was, and despite the fact that Aristotle had stated the very same idea as something of a supreme
command, I hadn't grasped it: *Oh, think about the real, actual*

audience? At no point during my speech preparation had it occurred to me to consider any of my fellow Toastmasters, what they might want to hear about, or how they might need to hear about it.

When I'd called my cousin Bill a few weeks earlier to tell him I'd joined Toastmasters, he'd mentioned that, in his opinion, shyness is little more than selfishness. "Call it modesty or bashfulness, if you will," he'd said. "But my underlying problem was thinking too much about myself and how others see me, instead of considering *them* and how *they* hear." I'd found his thoughts interesting, but surely they didn't apply to me. What could I possibly have in common with a recluse who'd lived in his parents' basement for forty-three years?

It dawned on me now just how this might be so: I'd gone to Toastmasters to learn what they teach, then spent more energy resisting their advice than absorbing it.

My Sahara speech had proven difficult because I'd deliberately picked a topic outside my audience's range of experience. The subject was highly interesting . . . *to me.* My second speech directed me to pay attention to organization, clarity, and transitions—subjects my audience had told me they cared about. I'd ignored the advice because their concerns didn't seem as interesting as my own.

And then I'd wondered why it was so hard to connect with these people.

3

GETTING TO THE POINT

One Friday in mid-August, five weeks after joining Toastmasters, I was sitting at my desk, waiting for a call from Toastmasters alumnus Tom Monaghan, founder of Domino's Pizza, former owner of the Detroit Tigers, and one of the richest men in the world.

Through high school friends, I'd found an office space tucked inside a dormer atop a Lutheran church near our apartment. The building was beautifully situated with a view of Lake of the Isles, a graceful, curving reservoir surrounded by running paths and stately villas from the early twentieth century. From my desk, through the window screen, I could see patches of water, near, far, hither and yon, ruffled by the breeze, rousing from placid slate to lively salt and pepper, then calming again. It looked as if the wind was playing tag with itself.

This was just the kind of pretty reverie I fall into when I'm traipsing toward depression, which, in fact, I was, thanks to the magnitude—and utter obviousness—of what I'd just learned. If the root of speech anxiety can accurately be diagnosed as a kind of selfishness (spoiler alert: it can be), and if the 74 percent of Americans afflicted with it might justly be described as suffering from an inability to see other people as real, actual people, it seemed like a profound indictment of how almost neurologically myopic we've become.

For a generation or so, social scientists have generated a ticker tape of alarming statistics charting the decline of America's social fabric. More than four in ten American adults report having "no one to confide in." Over a third of Americans say they "never" socialize with their neighbors (a figure that's risen 50 percent in the last forty years). A 2012 study conducted by scientists at the University of Michigan found that college students today demonstrate 40 percent less empathy than their peers from the 1980s. These trends, it seems, are mutually self-reinforcing. In a series of long-term studies by noted University of Chicago psychologist John Cacioppo, loneliness and self-centeredness feed off each other, creating a positive feedback loop: Our increased self-absorption leads to decreased skill at reading social cues, which then leads to an increase in social slights and mishaps, and hence to difficult, dissatisfying social relations. The harder we find social relations, the more we withdraw from them, further limiting opportunities to "practice" the skills of social relations.

It may well be that human nature is drastically changing, that once upon a time we were awesome, empathetic creatures and then modern life and the Internet came along and turned us into self-centered cretins who, coincidentally, are horrible at public speaking. But it's also possible (credible studies have challenged the accuracy of at least some of the findings above) that human beings have always been wretchedly unskilled at thinking of others. Such a conclusion squares nicely with the observation that ancient teachers of public speaking seemed as one in emphasizing empathy as the well-spring of eloquence.

While Aristotle remains rhetoric's greatest theorist, the world's most renowned and accessible *teacher* of the subject was a Roman statesman named Cicero. Widely admired as the greatest orator of his day, Cicero wrote not one but two books on rhetoric. The second, *De Oratore,* published in 55 B.C., remained a central text on the subject for the next fifteen centuries.

Like Aristotle, Cicero cared less for dispensing tips and rules about how to act like a confident speaker than enumerating a set of practical mental steps for getting out of one's head and focusing upon the audience. The first task of a public speaker, he wrote, is to "feel the people's pulse, whatever their kind, age, social class, [to] investigate the feelings of those [he] is going to speak to." Well before choosing a topic or making any other decision about how to give a speech, a speaker must "scent out with all possible keenness their thoughts, judgments, anticipations and wishes, and the direction in which they seem likely to be led away most easily by eloquence." No mention, one notes, of beta-blockers or imagining one's audience naked—nothing to do with the speaker themselves. The task of the orator, for Cicero, was to locate—on all levels, physical, spiritual, stylistic—the areas of commonality with an audience, a process he called "the art of connected terms."

Every audience, every topic, and every part and angle of every speech can be broken into constituent parts, approached from different angles, rearranged, reconceived, and rerelated to other parts and angles. Every idea has neighbors, relatives, a history, various components, and multiple shadings with multiple ways of being framed. Are you giving a speech to an audience that hates you? Or that loves you—but hates what you're about to propose? Are you shy, unsure of what to say? Find the thing, whatever it is—the subject, the *part* of a subject, the opposite of a subject, the history of the subject, or the fact that you and your audience are all wearing Gap jeans or are all Americans or all Midwesterners or all Republicans—that allows you to locate, then speak to, what is shared by you and your audience.

I'd glimpsed an appreciation of these ideas from my first two speeches, but my next Table Topic (about house music) proved as awkward as my speech about boots. "Think about the audience" sounded like a great idea. But after a lifetime of *not* thinking about the audience, it felt far from clear just how to do it, especially during an improvised speech exercise.

At 2:59, a minute early, the phone rang.

"Hello? Tom?"

"John? Hello!"

"Hi, Tom!"

Monaghan's amiable voice matched pictures I'd seen showing a man with a warm, easy smile and kind brown eyes—nothing like a feared denizen of the Fortune 500.

His rags-to-riches biography is often used as a business school parable. In 1960, he'd sold a VW Bug to buy a run-of-the-mill pizza parlor in Ann Arbor, Michigan, and proceeded to create the largest pizza chain in the United States. The firm today has a market capitalization of nearly $8 billion.

Less often told is the story of Monaghan's wrenching childhood. His father died when he was four, leaving his mother, a poorly paid domestic worker, unable to care for Monaghan and his brother. She'd deposited the brothers at an orphanage where boys were expected to dumpster-dive and beg for leftovers at restaurants. The hard-knocks upbringing left Monaghan severely handicapped by speech anxiety, a condition that plagued him into adulthood.

When I asked him to describe just how shy he'd been before joining Toastmasters, he sighed, saying, "Unbelievably shy. Painful. Particularly around women. The more I tried to be natural, the more spastic I got." With people he knew, he said, he described himself as acerbic, funny, and "socially normal." With strangers and larger groups, however, he froze. "Even in my own company," he said, "just asking a question at a meeting was tough." When I asked him how he forced himself to do so, he paused. "I avoided it."

By 1982, Domino's had grown to over 400 locations with a billion dollars in annual sales (the company would eventually boast over 5,000 stores worldwide). Naturally, an annual convention was in order, complete with an inspirational speech from the self-made CEO to fire up the legions of franchisees who'd gathered from around the world. "I found it absolutely petrifying," Monaghan told me. "I'd stand up there, reading from a piece of paper. I'd freeze. I'd lose my place," he said. "It was horrible."

Friends and colleagues had pushed him toward Toastmasters for years, but what finally prodded him to join, he told me, was the jealousy he felt when watching other CEOs taking pleasure in speaking about their companies. Monaghan was justly proud of what he'd built. Why shouldn't he be allowed to enjoy his role and celebrate its creation? Finally, in 1982, he joined two Toastmasters chapters, one within Domino's and another in Ypsilanti, Michigan.

"At my very first meeting," he said, "when they got to Table Topics, they called on me. They had my subject written on an index card. It said: 'Thinking Ahead.' So okay, I walked up to the podium. I looked out at everyone. And then I totally froze.

"I should have known plenty about the subject," he told me. "But the moment I looked out at the people, I couldn't think of a single thing to say." I could hear him swallow through the phone. "I was completely silent for the full two minutes," he said. "Everyone in the place was just aching for me, because I was supposedly a big deal by then."

When the bell went off, Monaghan made a wry joke. "Any questions?"

Funny. But probably not very fun.

At every meeting for the next five weeks, Monaghan volunteered for Table Topics, only to stammer and make scant improvement. On his sixth try, he received the following topic: "Name the person in your life who has had the most influence on you."

Monaghan recalled his childhood at the orphanage. The nuns had been unremittingly harsh disciplinarians. Except for one: Sister Mary Beranda. Beranda alone had been consistently kind—possibly providing the only warm memory of his childhood. She'd always helped him concentrate and pushed him to use his brain. He hadn't thought of her in years. As he remembered her sympathetic face and gentle voice, he felt a wave of gratitude. "I realized," he said, "that everything I have, I owe to her."

In that instant, Monaghan said, he found his voice. "Instead of fumbling around, pretending, like I usually did, the words just kinda flew out of my mouth." It helped that he felt positively and passionately about Sister Mary. But more important, he said, "For the first time at Toastmasters, I knew exactly what I wanted to get across. I wanted to brag to these people about what a tremendous person she was. It felt totally different than just babbling without knowing why you're talking." At meeting's end, he won the prize for Best Table Topic.

A week later, when I started working on my third speech, "Get to the Point," the lesson of Sister Mary stayed clearly in my mind. The instructions focused precisely upon the notion that Monaghan had touched on: the power of knowing *why* you're speaking before composing a speech.

My manual outlined a two-step process for defining my purpose. First, choose the general goal for the speech (most speeches aim to either inform, persuade, entertain, or inspire). Next, define the specific purpose. "As you plan a speech," my manual advised, "you must be absolutely clear about what you want the audience to do or know at the end of your talk." I should formulate a one-line sentence expressing the reaction I hoped to produce: "After hearing my speech, my audience will know X and will respond by doing Y."

The notion struck me as peculiar. Who was I to command a room full of people? I thought about the speeches I'd given throughout my life. Their general purpose had typically been *to inform*. To my mind, this meant something like copying a file from one hard drive to another. *At the end of my talk, my audience will know the same stuff I know.* The interaction, in my conception, was purely cerebral. It had nothing to do with telling anyone what to do.

My manual suggested choosing a mentor. As I'd begun to rein in my knee-jerk resistance to the club's teachings, I'd reached out to Gordon Andersen to ask him. After saying yes immediately, Andersen suggested treating my speeches like simple technical exercises, rather than opportunities to express the furthest reaches of my soul. He used the analogy of a musician playing scales. Indeed, when I focused on the technical lesson of each exercise and set aside the desire to be profound and meaningful, I seemed to learn more and struggle less.

While continuing to devour Greek and Roman writings on rhetoric, I'd also discovered public speaking manuals from around the world. The Greeks and Romans didn't seem to mention it, but other cultures often stressed the importance of knowing when *not* to talk. Confucius, for example, regarded clever talk as a sign of weakness and extolled silence as the highest form of eloquence. Buddhism counseled that speech should be used sparingly, solely as a means for advancing truth and love. Numerous writings on statecraft, courtroom conduct, and meeting protocol from Egypt to Bali likewise emphasized the importance of speaking only when one's opinion was desired.

Public speaking had been taught for eons using a variety of conceptual frameworks. Surveying the diversity of approaches to the subject had helped me better understand my antipathy toward the Dale Carnegie rah-rah school of public speaking. It wasn't just that "acting confident" seemed insincere, but that its near-universal adoption as a one-size-fits-all strategy to the wildly complex, nearly existential issue of how we carry ourselves through a noisy, bustling world ignored other approaches that seemed a better fit for shy, self-aware people averse to behaving inauthentically. These older, more thoughtful methods seemed to suggest a variety of pathways toward eloquence.

My *general purpose,* I decided, would be to inform my fellow Toastmasters that the rah-rah school of public speaking is not the only path to eloquence. My *specific purpose* would be to urge my audience to consider silence—or other low-key alternatives to fake peppiness—as an overlooked tool for effective communication.

I titled my speech "Shut Up."

My manual suggested that sharpening my purpose would make my speech easier to write. "Each time you edit your speech," it advised, "all other decisions relating to your speech—what information to include, organization and delivery—are easy to make, since you will measure them against their helpfulness in achieving your purpose."

Indeed, within moments of defining my specific purpose, the writing became surprisingly easy. Where in the past I would have spent hours weighing the merits of every idea, word choice, and sentence, it now felt easy to see what was relevant and what wasn't. I finished the speech in record time.

The manual also promised that focusing the purpose of my speech would reduce my nervousness about delivering it. I didn't believe that for a second. On the evenings of my two previous speeches, I'd arrived at the Byerly's parking lot one minute before the start of the meeting, then lingered in the car until the last possible second, dreading the humiliations waiting for me inside the community room. Now, for the first time since I'd joined the club, my pre-speech jitters felt almost manageable. As I walked through the supermarket, passing the bright lights and busy shoppers, I felt nervous, but not nauseous. When the meeting got to speech time, I felt ready.

I introduced my speech with thirty seconds of silence (I'd discover later that this was also one of Hitler's favorite ways to begin a speech). It was kind of fun, in an Andy Kaufman, make-your-audience-squirm sort of way. I crossed purposefully from one side of the room to the other, keeping my eye on my fellow Toastmasters in a way I hoped telegraphed something more like slyness than psychosis. It was, to be sure, a testy way to begin a speech. But I'd definitely grabbed my clubmates' attention. No one made a sound.

"Madam Toastmaster, fellow Toastmasters, and distinguished guests," I began:

> From Dale Carnegie to Toastmasters, Americans are taught that the best way to speak in public is to be likable. Confident. That the road to good communication is paved with smiles. And lots of words. I'd like to suggest that there is another way to reach people which is possibly more honest. Less stressful. And less annoying.

I would offer, I explained, three examples demonstrating the power of verbal restraint.

The first was about an ex-girlfriend who'd devised an unusual trick for defusing tensions. In the run-up to an argument, just as one of us approached exasperation with the other, she'd pause and say, with equal measures of warmth and irony, "I love you." The words functioned as a rhetorical off-ramp, a fuse short-circuiting any impulse to continue bickering. It almost always worked. (After all, how do you argue with someone who says, "I love you?")

In the second story, I related a trick I learned from a high-powered corporate attorney who specialized in negotiating multi-billion-dollar, multi-party settlements. When a counterparty demanded something particularly unreasonable, in lieu of countering with an indignant, well-reasoned rebuttal, he'd learned to simply ask, "Wait. I don't understand. Can you please repeat that?" He told me with a chuckle that even the most outrageously greedy negotiators tend to run out of steam by the third time they're forced to explain an untenably selfish position.

My final example cited President Barack Obama's State of the Union address, televised the night before. I'd obtained a transcript and run a word count: 6,419 words. By comparison, Lincoln's Gettysburg Address comes in at 272. Obama's speech wasn't bad. But it wasn't twenty-four times better than the Gettysburg Address.

Brevity, people.

In closing, I repeated what I'd said earlier:

> We, especially Toastmasters, invest a lot of energy in learning to speak well. Perhaps we might communicate more effectively if we also considered the possibility of speaking less.

On the final beat of the speech, I found myself smiling at my fellow Toastmasters. I hadn't forced it. I wasn't trying to act like they were my friends. I simply felt relieved and pleased with myself. I'd followed the instructions (finally) and they'd worked like a charm. Andersen smiled as my clubmates clapped for me, and while I can't be sure, it seemed as though their posture and eye contact had indicated a slightly higher degree of engagement than they might had my speech been awful. For the first time in my life, my body had been in the same room as my voice and brain and a group of strangers. I'd "been myself" and said what I'd meant to say in the way that I'd meant to say it. In short: I'd connected. All I'd had to do was think about who I was talking to and why. It sounds like nothing. It felt like rocket science.

At the end of the meeting, Margo Forster, the elderly

woman in white tennis shoes who'd told the Sven and Ole joke at my first meeting, evaluated my speech. She praised my organization and said my purpose was clear from beginning to end. Delivery-wise, not so much. I needed to project more consistently and expressively, and to get my hands out of my pockets. I was still balling them up into fists. In conclusion, she said, despite my slightly ornery topic, I'd done a great job and I was coming along nicely.

I was so dazed from the novelty of giving a speech without feeling flattened by anxiety or shame, I barely heard her. I felt high.

The meeting ended, and as I gathered my pen, notebook, and recorder, I overheard a new member named Hanna Turnquist telling an even newer member named Kelly, "Toastmasters is changing my personality." I must have signaled my curiosity, because she and Kelly shifted slightly to make room for me. I asked her what she meant, and she said, "It's making me nicer."

Turnquist, a brown-haired, casually dressed, thirty-something engineer, worked as an IT project manager for a pharmacy benefits management company. She spent her days coordinating technical operations, then relaying her team's results to her superiors. "I'd always imagined," she said, "that my job in meetings is to rattle off my numbers as fast as possible and get out of the way." Now, she said, "I realize that even phone meetings are a kind of public speaking. You're saying words out loud to an audience. And the same rules apply. You have to think about who you're talking to and why. If people just wanted numbers, you'd send it by email. The reason you get on the phone and have a live conversation is to create rapport."

It made sense. But how, I asked, had this insight made her *nicer*?

"I've started to think more about people instead of just facts and numbers and stuff," she said. "You know, did they just get divorced? Maybe they just got a promotion. It sounds corny, but when I think about the real purpose of why we're talking, it forces me to remember what's important in life. Like, hey, we're alive! We're not robots!"

Between us and the door, Laura Betz, the tall, exhausted-looking Chinese woman (who, I'd learned, was obtaining a PhD in pharmacy while raising a family), stood talking to Brad Gadjus, a gangly young stock clerk. Gordon Andersen sat chatting with Magool Dirie, a thirty-something Somali law student attending her second meeting. Antonia Grefa, a middle-aged social worker from Ecuador, was talking to Alex Čapek.

In an era in which, according to the Pew Research Center, 96 percent of Americans own a cellphone and 81 percent own a smartphone—when 28 percent of American adults and roughly half of eighteen-to-twenty-nine-year-olds report being online "almost constantly"—this disparate group of people, who would never otherwise meet, had joined a club to learn how to talk to one another better. Consciously or not, they'd left their screens behind to immerse themselves in the mechanics of interacting in the actual, physical world using their senses, vibes, prana, presence. As I'd observe in deepening waves, this seemingly geeky club and its largely forgotten subject had profound implications, offering the most subtle, relevant form of education I'd ever encountered.

"You know?" said Turnquist, as we reached the door. "I guess it's making me more human."

For weeks after my conversation with Turnquist, I continued to reflect upon the exercise. I've always thought of myself as being empathetic. And maybe I am—one-on-one. But I'd never considered what it means with a group. My former concept of giving a speech—that I'm a disc drive, copying my data to other disc drives—consisted of me taking a stage and disgorging my information as quickly as possible while defending myself against the stares of the audience members, as if the exchange of information was the priority and they themselves were something of an inconvenience. Asking myself "What do I want them to know or do as a result of my speech?" reframed the occasion as a social interaction, rather than a strained, robotic, one-way communication from me to them. In the most transformative way imaginable, thinking about my purpose for speaking completed the command to "think about the audience." The implications of the exercise extended well beyond my Speakeasy meetings.

From sociologist Erwin Goffman in the 1950s to linguists Penelope Brown and Stephen Levinson in the 1980s and '90s and cognitive psychologist Steven Pinker in the 2000s, scientists specializing in communication have described speech as vastly less devoted to conveying information than to managing our social status. Pinker, in his 2007 book *The Stuff of Thought,* demonstrates the following ways we can ask for a helping of guacamole:

I was wondering if you could pass the guacamole.
Do you think you could pass the guacamole?
If you could pass the guacamole, that would be awesome.

Why, he asks, do we avoid, ignore, eschew, and otherwise tiptoe around more straightforward ways of saying the same thing, like "Pass the guacamole" or "Pass the guacamole, please"? Because, he answers, it's through the "I was wondering"'s and "Do you think"'s—the indirect, "noninformational" components of speech—that we attempt to massage others' perceptions of us. Quoting Samuel Johnson ("No two men can be half an hour together but one shall acquire an evident superiority over the other"), Pinker explains that these seeming detours from efficiency are the means by which we pursue the deeper, truer social goals of speech.

The takeaway, for me, was not that we lard our speech with curlicues and addenda offering clues about who we really are, nor that we simultaneously speak on two levels at once, one direct and one indirect. Most adults, no doubt, are aware of what I'm noting. The point—and this would be true for virtually every principle of communication I would learn—was how profitable the lesson became when applied rigorously, literally, and consciously. What would happen if I—if we—asked ourselves more often, in everyday conversation, "What do I want my listener to do or say as a result of my speech?"

In 1975, a British-educated philosopher of language named Paul Grice produced a seminal paper introducing what have become known as Grice's Maxims, a set of four theoretical principles binding good conversation:

Quantity: Say no less or more than the conversation requires. Be as informative as possible—don't over-inform.

Quality: Say nothing you believe to be false. Say nothing for which you lack evidence.

Manner: Be clear, orderly, and brief. Avoid obscurity and ambiguity.

Relevance: Be relevant.

Grice's Maxims are largely observed in the breach. We talk too little, too much, we veer off topic, overemphasizing unimportant details while skipping past essentials. We cite facts we've never verified and state opinion as established truth. Such transgressions notwithstanding, in an overall theory called the Cooperative Principle, Grice maintained that the underlying precept of conversation is a kind of relentless rationality: speakers *always* have a point, no matter how indirectly they make it; listeners always *assume* they have a point—and strive to interpret everything a speaker says as relevant.

Grice's precepts sound both modern and quasi-scientific, but the Cooperative Principle simply echoes Aristotle: There is always a reason why we speak, and that reason is to persuade. At a minimum, we want people to like, understand, and believe us—and not, for example, to check their phones or walk away from us in midsentence. The idea reappears in Cicero and in the writings of Kenneth Burke (a twentieth-century literary and rhetorical theorist who held that every noise, call, chirp, or sign made by every animal on earth is an attempt to influence other animals), Dale Carnegie, and Ralph C. Smedley, the latter two both stating, "All speech is sales"—a turn of phrase I found reductive and off-putting before eventually agreeing with it.

I wondered: If (a) speakers always have a point; (b) that point is essentially and above all an attempt to manage or enhance our social status; and (c) the most valuable, presumably status-enhancing ingredient of conversation is ultimately relevance, then why aren't we taught to ask ourselves more often why we're speaking?

———

Isabel, Santi, and I had entered a loose rhythm of dining twice a week at my mother's twentieth-floor apartment, three floors above ours but infinitely more elegant. We'd sit in her mid-century modern chairs, flanked by her late-twentieth-century South American paintings, eating gourmet meals she cranked out, at age eighty-two, after working four days a week. One evening in late August, on the birthday I share with her, we were joined by my songwriter/music producer brother, who lived two miles away, and by my copywriter sister, who flew in from New York.

My mother has always driven my siblings and me crazy with non sequiturs. If I said, "I'm going to Georgia for work," my mom might say, "Maybe you'll run into Tiger." If time and circumstance permitted and I had time to unpack my mother's reply (which doesn't happen after you have a baby), I might find out that sometime in the early 1960s, my mom and dad attended the Masters golf tournament in Augusta. In her mind, then, Georgia = golf, golf = Tiger (as in Woods), and the link between Georgia and Tiger makes perfect sense. Her remarks tend to carom off others' comments more often than relating to them.

My brother, meanwhile, had always been a keen listener, but found it difficult not to steer conversations to the subject of his career (he's the first to admit this). If I mentioned, "I've been listening to a lot of Arcade Fire lately," he might cite a song of theirs; note the production sound of, say, the song's snare drum; and then segue to, "That's funny. I'm producing a CD for this rockabilly-EDM band from Chicago and we used that exact same snare drum sound." And then he'd be off and running about his music. My sister, probably the best listener and talker among us, had developed, over the years, the teacherly habit of calling us out for repeating ourselves and offering unsolicited advice about how we might speak more clearly or correctly. She was right more often than not, but the habit had made me reluctant to speak my mind in her presence.

Suffice it to say the Bowe clan had yet to master the art of connection. I'd learned, over the decades, to enjoy my family's wit and erudition; but I'd also learned to tamp down my expectations of deriving great emotional satisfaction from conversations with them.

As we enjoyed our celebratory meal, I found myself deploying my newfound analytical skills. Like any form of neurotic behavior, my family's disjointed conversational habits appeared to be driven by unexamined emotional needs. My mother's non sequiturs were quite possibly motivated by an urge to demonstrate her worldliness (funny, because she's fluent in five languages and is among the worldliest people I know). My brother's obsessive regression to the topic of his work seemed fueled by a desire to be known and understood by the people he loves (funny again, because after twenty-eight years, he's one of the most happily married people I know). My sister's habit of criticizing might perhaps have been driven by a need to be perceived as intelligent (funny one more time, because everyone I know finds her remarkably perceptive and sharp). How much more emotionally satisfying might our conversations be if they questioned their purpose for speaking as they did?

Having analyzed everyone else's linguistic peccadilloes, I turned my magnifying glass on myself. Since childhood, I'd endured our group conversations by staying in my lane as the baby of the family, floating along self-protectively, lobbing quick, low-risk ripostes and cute one-offs while venturing little of real substance, and meanwhile rolling my eyes (to myself) and feeling superior for remaining aloof from their self-absorbed, attention-seeking ways.

I now saw at a glance the childishness of my stance; it was every bit as neurotic and connection-averse as my family members'. I understood why I'd assumed a defensive conversational crouch. But still, if, as Aristotle, Pinker, and Grice had suggested, my behavior must nevertheless have had a purpose, conscious or not, what was it? What was I trying to say, despite my hesitance about saying it?

Several years earlier, I'd been hired to write a biography about a man whom I'll call Phil. Phil suffered from Tourette syndrome and obsessive-compulsive disorder. The Tourette's manifested in conjunction with severe OCD, causing him not only to twitch or "tic" but to jerk his neck, make barking noises, and compulsively seek out the most risky, offensive behavior in unfamiliar situations. In high school, Phil would pass by classmates and blurt, "You're fat!" or "I wanna fuck you!" He'd been arrested in the Indianapolis bus station for repeatedly shouting racial slurs. In an airport security line he once began yelling, "Bomb, bomb, bomb!" (His book, by the way, was not about overcoming his harrowing, embarrassing malady, but about learning the meaning of tolerance shown him by the people he'd constantly offended.)

When I met him, he'd been talking for half an hour with my friend Jamie. When I arrived, Jamie, who is gay, snickered and said, "This guy's called me faggot eight times already! I can't wait to hear what he's gonna call you."

Two weeks later, Phil and I were on the West Side Highway, driving from New York City to upstate New York to begin working on his life story. It was the first time we'd been alone together. As I drove, I could almost feel him going crazy, as if he were a psychic Geiger counter, searching for my

weak spot, the chink in my armor where my pride or preten-
tions might leave me vulnerable to insult. He searched and
searched. At length, I began to feel pretty good about myself.
Apparently, I had no weak spots or pretensions for him to assault.

Suddenly, he began ticcing: "I'm bored! I'm! Bored!
Bored!"

It took me a day to understand—or, rather, to admit to
myself—why he'd chosen this particular tack to offend me. If
there was a subtext to everything I said and did, it was that I
wanted everyone to know I was interesting. It's why, for example, I'd found it necessary to speak about my travels across
the Sahara Desert instead of something closer to home and
more relatable to my fellow Toastmasters. It's why I'd found it
so hard to follow the Toastmasters directions for organizing a
speech. It seemed to me more important to demonstrate how
unique I was than to let go of my ego and follow their lead.
It also explained my disinclination to engage deeply in family
conversations. Confronted with a situation so inauspicious for
demonstrating my superior creativity and uniqueness, I simply surrendered. Perhaps silence and aloofness might signal
my cleverness more than anything I might say.

My sin—wanting people to notice at every turn that I'm
the most interesting guy around—amounted to a garden-
variety form of cluelessness, both about myself and the nature
of good communication. Looking at it clearly, as a budding
rhetorician on his forty-eighth birthday with a baby in his
arms and a partner by his side, I reflected upon how *I* feel
when people hijack the shared space of conversation for their
own self-centered needs instead of acknowledging me and
talking to me (as opposed to prattling). I realized with a gulp
I'd been every bit as guilty as everyone around me. So what

would my daily interactions be like if I let go of the blind, constant impulse to prove how original I was? I'd have to work harder to find subjects other people cared about. But that would probably be less alienating than showing off and trying to win points for being clever. Would I find it easier to connect with people if I thought a bit more about them, and less about myself?

Turnquist was right. And so were Isocrates, Aristotle, and Cousin Bill. If eloquence still seemed very far away, this odd, innocent little exercise in learning how to give a speech was beginning to have a profound effect on my thinking.

4

YOU KIND OF MELLOW OUT

n a 2001 essay called "Tense Present: Democracy, English, and the Wars over Usage," the writer David Foster Wallace describes the following quandary:

> Suppose that you and I are acquaintances and we're in my apartment having a conversation and that at some point I want to terminate the conversation and not have you be in my apartment anymore. Very delicate social moment. Think of all the different ways I can try to handle it: "Wow, look at the time"; "Could we finish this up later?"; "Could you please leave now?"; "Go"; "Get out"; "Get the hell out of here"; "Didn't you say you had to be someplace?"; "Time for you to hit the dusty trail, my friend"; "Off you go then, love"; or that sly old telephone-conversation-ender, "Well, I'm going to let you go now"; etc. etc.
>
> ... In real life I always seem to have a hard time winding up a conversation or asking somebody to leave, and

sometimes the moment becomes so delicate and fraught with social complexity that I'll get overwhelmed . . . and will just sort of blank out and do it totally straight—"I want to terminate the conversation and not have you be in my apartment anymore"—which evidently makes me look either as if I'm very rude and abrupt or as if I'm semi-autistic. . . . I've actually lost friends this way.

Wallace's inner hysteria may seem amusingly neurotic, all too familiar, or both. What I find fascinating about the passage is the role it highlights between word choice ("Think of all the different ways I can try to handle it") and mental health. At the risk of being obvious: When we choose words well, we are not only judged to be "nice," "pleasant," "easy to get along with," "smart," and so forth, we are also judged to be healthy, normal, functional, and sane. When we choose words that are vague, inappropriate, or offensive, we are labeled hard to understand, difficult, or downright hostile, and ultimately run the risk of being labeled neurotic, damaged, dumb, or mentally ill. Choice by choice, one interaction at a time, our words determine our social relationships, and consequently whether our lives will be happy and fulfilled or lonely and depressing.

From a modern perspective, people who speak offensively, like Wallace's "semi-autistic," do so because something's *psychologically* wrong with them. It would seem unscientific and slightly balmy to suggest that speech is the problem, much less the solution to the problem, because as we know, psychological issues stem from something gone awry *deep inside of us.*

The Greeks, I'd learned, approached the relationship between speech and mental health from a completely different angle. By way of example, *aporein,* the fourth-century B.C.

word for "embarrassment," meant neither timidity nor bash-fulness nor anything so emotional but, rather, "perplexity or hesitation," meaning, literally, "to have no way out." Shyness, in other words, had less to do with psychology, brain chemi-cals, or character traits than it did with a deficit of language and social skills. In the same way that a young soldier lacking military training could hardly be branded a coward for run-ning from battle, a person lacking speech training could hardly be deemed mentally ill.

The Greeks viewed rhetoric and speech training as the es-sential social educational process, for shaping both fully formed humans and a fully functional society. Learning to speak meant acquiring skill and poise at using words; but it also meant learning to analyze all sides of an argument be-fore forming and expressing one's opinion. Like reading and writing today, it was a comprehensive critical approach to knowledge—with an additional, insistent emphasis on psy-chology and social interaction. Implicit to ancient curricula was a heightened understanding that all knowledge, even sci-entific knowledge, is, by way of being presented (by *someone*), grounded in a point of view.

From Aristotle's time through the medieval period, pupils, beginning at age twelve, were guided through what today seems like a breathtakingly commonsense, fourteen-step, multi-year curriculum of speech exercises known as the *pro-gymnasmata*. Beginning by reciting short, memorized stories for their classmates, students progressed to longer, more intri-cate narratives featuring multiple personae. By acting out the voices of story characters—good, bad, young, old, strong, and weak—pupils absorbed through practice the poetic, mu-sical, rhythmic, and theatrical components of effective speech. Later exercises encouraged them to sharpen their critical abilities and argumentation skills, to author their own points of view in speeches of praise and condemnation about current events and politicians. By the time they reached what we'd call high school, students could extemporize for an hour straight after five minutes' preparation, holding forth on topics of staggering complexity, such as "What makes government good or bad?" and "Which is superior: town life or country life?"

Odd as the notion may seem today, shyness, introversion, and keeping to oneself were practically forbidden, at least among the educated classes. Early democracy had proven prey to plots, coups, and upheaval; the success of self-rule required full participation. Sitting on the sidelines and avoiding debate was considered not just bad manners or social anxiety, but a potential sign of ill intent against the community.

Rhetoric classes well into the sixteenth century almost uniformly included the cautionary tale of the famous general Lyncestes, who was accused of conspiracy against Alexander the Great. Brought before a military tribunal to defend himself, Lyncestes stuttered and stammered. His guards, growing weary of waiting for an answer, were at length obliged to stab him with their pikes, thus terminating his protracted defense. The mores of the day were unironically clear: educated adults know how to use their tongues. If Lyncestes had been innocent, he would have found the words to say so.

My fourth Toastmasters exercise, "How to Say It," emphasized the importance of choosing words that work well specifically in the context of a speech. The manual's instructions were simple enough: Write a speech expressing your ideas with vivid, precise language.

Listeners in a live setting have only one opportunity to hear your words and comprehend their meaning—all the while tuning out multiple sources of distraction. The best way to help them hear you well is to use short words, short sentences, and short paragraphs. You can further aid their comprehension by translating abstract concepts into concrete nouns, using colorful images that appeal to the senses, and replacing passive verbs and boring expressions with more energetic alternatives.

I'd begun, thanks to the Ah Counter report at the end of every meeting, to prune my speech of wasteful filler words like "umm," "y'know," "kind of," "sort of," "I mean," and so on. My manual offered several additional ways to cleanse, purify, and intensify my speech. Instead of saying "about six," "five or six," or "half a dozen," say *"six."* Instead of using flabby jargon words like "utilize" or "implement," choose the simplest terms possible, like "use" or "start."

Further, it explained: Be specific. Words like "large," "rich," "cheap," "dog," or even "brown" work fine in everyday conversation with friends and family sharing similar frames of reference. Their meaning, however, becomes vague and even counterproductive when speaking to a diverse audience. If "a large house" might mean 3,500 square feet to a wealthy person from suburban Arizona but 500 square feet to a working-class visitor from Tokyo, you're better off specifying exactly how many square feet you mean. Speech works best when everyone hearing it understands and feels the same thing—together—which is, of course, the power of public speaking.

For my "How to Say It" exercise, I searched for a subject rich with powerful, expressive images and quickly (if not too subtly) decided on the attack on the World Trade Center on September 11, 2001. My home in New York at that time was less than a mile away. I wrote a speech describing a meal I had with my sister and a food critic friend at a fancy midtown restaurant three days after the attack. The world around us had (rightly) stopped functioning, but, nevertheless, the critic had a deadline to meet. Thus, at a time when most New Yorkers had no idea how to move forward with their lives, the invitation to spend a few hours sharing a free, luxurious meal came as a welcome distraction.

The topic offered plenty of opportunities to create images appealing to the senses. I described the purple glow of the restaurant's recessed fluorescent ceiling lights; the piney, mineral notes of the white Burgundy wine; the frequent, surreal rumble of sci-fi-looking supersonic patrol jets roaring overhead in tight formation, rattling the windows. I'd saved the strongest language for the end of the story: when we exited the restaurant, murmuring our appreciation for the outlandishly rich meal, the wind, courtesy of Osama bin Laden, carried to our noses an odor we'd never before encountered—the smell of human flesh and toxic chemicals wafting from the charred towers. Morbid, yes—but definitely vivid.

I'll skip the blow-by-blow depiction of how my speech went. It wasn't perfect. I'd leaped so enthusiastically at the task of creating memorable, punchy images, I'd forgotten to pause and define the purpose of the speech. Having failed to "aim" it toward my audience, I'd slipped back toward my earlier, more self-centered approach, unconsciously trying to demonstrate, once again, how interesting I was, this time via my gruesome word choices. Slightly daunted by how easily I'd relapsed, I took comfort in the fact that the speech still went okay. For the second time in a row—for the second time in my life—I managed to stand and talk to a group of people without feeling awful.

I'm sure that in previous, pre-Toastmasters speeches, I'd deployed concrete images and tried my best to use words efficiently. But I'd never been taught to think systematically about how people listen in a live context. While I couldn't measure the exact degree to which my improved word choices had resonated with my group, it seemed reasonable to surmise that by cutting the 20 percent or so of my words that were entirely unnecessary, I'd made my speech 20 percent more potent—and more connected. Using concrete images versus abstract concepts felt more connected as well; when I described the roar of a jet overhead, they knew exactly what I meant.

My evaluator that meeting was Al Hoffman—he of the many-pocketed bird-watching vest. He praised me for using short, simple words, vivid images, and compressed phrasings, for memorizing my speech and making good eye contact. He criticized me for tensing up and balling my hands into fists and jamming them into my pockets (still!) and for lacking a clear purpose. Overall, he concluded, I was coming along nicely.

As he began to evaluate the speaker who'd followed me, I found myself drifting off. I mentioned earlier that Hoffman was exceedingly meek. His timidity was the first thing you noticed about him. It wasn't the kind of red-faced awkwardness that forces bystanders to feel uncomfortable, but a particularly Midwestern brand of self-effacing blandness that caused him to come across as a near-total cipher. One of the newer members, a funny younger guy, had quipped, "Al's not exactly a great advertisement for Toastmasters." At first, I'd agreed. Hoffman had been a member of Speakeasy since 1978, but in some ways, he seemed the shyest guy in the room.

But over the course of several chats, as I learned about

Hoffman's life, marriage, and kids, I also began to appreciate the magnitude of what Toastmasters had done for him. In the 1970s, he'd taken a job in the data entry department at a national insurance and financial products company. Smart, quick, and good with numbers, Hoffman excelled, but he described his struggle with what he called "the social parts of the job." "I was just real paranoid about aggravating people by saying the wrong thing," he explained. In 1984, a sympathetic supervisor urged him to join Toastmasters. Two years later, Hoffman got promoted into management. Two years after that, he got married. As I'd seen and marveled at several times already, Toastmasters had produced for Hoffman the kind of transformation often sought through expensive, long-term therapy. As Hoffman aptly explained, "When you learn to stop and think about your words from the other person's point of view, you kinda mellow out. You learn to move through awkward situations." His words called to mind the distinction my cousin Bill had made, explaining that Toastmasters hadn't cured him of shyness; it had taught him a method for connecting *despite* his shyness.

Hoffman spoke often—almost every time we talked— about losing a 1986 election for a volunteer position with the local parks board. Thirty years after the fact, he seemed gently obsessed, unable to let go of the loss. Between the election and fragments I'd gleaned about his childhood and family, I wondered if maybe he suffered from depression. Or something. Still, whatever it was, Hoffman led a more active and integrated social life than most people I know. Enjoying his retirement, he belonged to several organizations, one of which he called his "harmonica club." Every Monday, he and a group of mates donned what he called "our harmonica uniforms" and visited area rest homes to play old standards like

"You Are My Sunshine," "My Bonnie Lies Over the Ocean," and "Take Me Out to the Ballgame" (he explained that these are the only songs that octogenarians remember through the fog of Alzheimer's, dementia, and advanced age). "It's fun," he said. "We have a Chinese girl who comes. She plays three harmonicas at once!"

Hoffman showed up to Toastmasters meetings week after week wearing his vest—its dozen-plus pockets stuffed to overflowing with pens, manuals, guides, and cards with Table Topics ideas written on them—serving, despite his quirks, as a stalwart model of "active participation," delivering Jokes of the Week, Table Topics, and prepared speeches while volunteering for a variety of club officer positions. Whenever events threatened the flow of a meeting (say, a Table Topicsmaster failed to arrive to perform their duties, or three speakers received the same number of votes for best Joke of the Week), Hoffman, shy or not, always seemed to know what to do and say to keep the meeting moving along.

As I'd gotten to know Toastmasters like Hoffman, Roy Chenier, Susan Cain, and my cousin Bill and observed the ways they'd learned to connect with others, I'd come to view the fact that (according to the National Institutes of Health) 74 percent of Americans suffer from speech anxiety as more than a mere statistic. The number seemed to hint (or rather shout) at the degree to which we've lost the ability to "think our words through from other people's point of view." The Pew Research Center found that 47 percent of smartphone owners between eighteen and twenty-nine years old use their phone "to avoid interacting with the people around them." Another survey found that fewer than one in four Americans speak with people with whom they disagree politically. Such findings raised a nuanced question: Has technology caused people to become shyer, more socially isolated, more over-sensitive, and less adept at the art of politics, engagement, and compromise? Or have citizens retreated into their techno-logical devices because modern education no longer teaches them how to connect with other humans?

I found food for thought in Harvard political scientist Robert Putnam's groundbreaking study of American social connectedness, *Bowling Alone*. Two decades ago, Putnam tracked the rise and near demise of American civic life. From the founding of the American colonies, he discovered, Americans belonged to political, church, and social groups with a level of civic enthusiasm unmatched anywhere in the world. From the 1970s through the publication of his book in 2000, however, by every measure, participation in American civic life plummeted. Voting: down by a fifth. Involvement with clubs, party politics, religious social organizations outside of worship: down by 40 percent or more. Through the 1960s, Putnam found, the vast majority of Americans engaged in one or more forms of civic engagement every year. From 1994 onward, however, the majority did not engage in any. Equally discouraging, studies found that the plummeting levels of civic participation mirrored dwindling interest in public affairs and diminishing trust in government and neighbors.

"For the first two-thirds of the twentieth century," Putnam continues, "a powerful tide bore Americans into ever deeper engagement in the life of their communities." But somehow, in the last few decades, "silently, without warning—that tide reversed and we were overtaken by a treacherous rip current. Without at first noticing, we have been pulled apart from one another and from our communities."

The "crumbling of social connectedness" described by Putnam corresponds neatly with what journalist Bill Bishop calls "ideological inbreeding," the increasing tendency over the last few decades for Americans to relocate to neighborhoods where people share their skin color, economic class, and political and religious persuasions. "Today," Bishop concludes, "most Americans live in communities that are becoming more politically homogeneous and, in effect, diminish dissenting views. And that grouping of like-minded people is feeding the nation's increasingly rancorous and partisan politics."

Quoting John Stuart Mill ("It is hardly possible to overrate the value . . . of placing human beings in contact with persons dissimilar to themselves, and with modes of thought and action unlike those with which they are familiar"), Putnam continues, "Joiners become more tolerant, less cynical, and more empathetic to the misfortunes of others. Mixing with people different than ourselves moderates our views and restrains us from our worst impulses."

Putnam and Bishop explore a variety of potential causes for America's social fragmentation, from suburban sprawl to the Internet, the disintegration of the traditional family, rising wealth inequality, and changing work patterns. While no single explanation emerges as the sole cause, Putnam did find that the roots of virtually every antisocial trend he studied had established themselves well before the rise of the Internet. So much for blaming Twitter. But what about TV?

David Foster Wallace had some thoughts about that. Examining the effect of television on American culture in his 1993 essay, "E Unibus Pluram: TV and U.S. Fiction," Wallace homed in on the enervating influence of comedic irony, pioneered by *Saturday Night Live* (which launched in 1975) and *Late Night with David Letterman* (1982). Following on the heels of the political disappointments and disillusioning events of the 1960s and 1970s—the Vietnam War, the assassinations of the Kennedys and Martin Luther King, Jr., the Nixon administration's Watergate scandal—these shows exerted an almost incalculable influence, entertaining millions of fans with a cool, knowing mockery of formerly sacrosanct institutions: the government, organized religion, corporations, and so on.

The civically disengaged Americans chronicled by Putnam had dedicated themselves to watching TV (at the time of Wallace's writing) for six hours a day, immersing themselves in a perpetual, collaborative denial of reality—namely, that *Yes, while you and millions of others are watching these shows under the guidance and control of our advertisers, you, my friend, are no one's dupe. You are in on the joke.* "The joke" was that taking things too seriously was for suckers.

Wallace had no beef with television. He loved it. But he bemoaned the conversion of millions of Americans to its new religion of ironic mocking, irreverence, what-the-fuck shoulder-shrugging, and persistent distancing from real troubles, real despair, and problems of political and corporate corruption. As Wallace saw it, viewers had become increasingly invested in their onscreen relationships and decreasingly able—or willing—to handle "the psychic costs of being around other humans."

The heart of Wallace's lament zeroed in on a kind of voicelessness. As a nation of cynical entertainment addicts, allergic to earnestness and sincerity, we'd become wary to the point of paranoia of taking stands, about saying what we mean. *If I say what I mean, I might be wrong. I might be stupid. You might laugh at me.* Irony's mass adoption, Wallace feared, had proved a cul-de-sac of self- and political expression, a "grim solution" to the political, economic, and spiritual problems facing America, and an "agent of a great despair and stasis in US culture." To Wallace, it seemed we'd gotten stuck.

What would it take to rouse Americans from the slough of ironic despond? At his conclusion, he imagines a new breed of cultural renegade, willing to speak up and to take on "the psychic costs of being around other humans." These upstarts would be hardy enough to speak their minds, braving yawns, rolled eyes, and accusations of naïveté. "Real rebels, as far as I can see," he writes, "risk things. Risk disapproval."

I read Wallace's essay for the first time twenty years before joining Toastmasters. Upon reading it again now, I found myself reflected in its indictment. I'd grown up squarely within his TV-watching demographic with the jaundiced view that people—especially people standing before lecterns—who earnestly profess their beliefs are suspect. *They're showing off. They're lying. They're trying to get something.* I sat on the sidelines, voiceless, too smart, too cool, too jaded to state my opinion—while proudly imagining myself a rebel. Was I emotionally, spiritually, or politically smarter than the rest of the world for knowing that most of what people say in public is ultimately bullshit? Or, as I wondered now, was I simply unskilled and terrified about speaking up in general in the same way I was reluctant to talk at the family dinner table? In both cases, I realized, I blamed the world for communicating badly instead of looking for a way to engage.

I began to wonder: What if the reason for America's civic and social malaise had less to do with its populace becoming cynical, withdrawn, and intolerant and more to do with our general ignorance about public speaking?

One night in September I was cooking dinner with Isabel at my mother's apartment, making shakshuka (we'd decided maybe *we* should cook for *her*), when my phone rang. The caller was Debbi Fields Rose, the world's most successful purveyor of fresh cookies. I'd been advised she would call, but nevertheless found myself surprised and thrilled to hear her warm, musical voice coming over the phone. "Hey, John! Is this a good time to talk?"

Fields Rose launched Mrs. Fields Cookies in 1977, expanded it to include some 650 franchises around the world, then sold it in the early 1990s for an estimated $400 million. Of all the Toastmasters I would interview, she seemed the least shy. From the founding days of her company, Fields Rose, now in her mid-sixties, has been the company spokeswoman, a bubbly, outgoing person known to her friends as "the Energizer Bunny."

Stepping out to the balcony, I asked her why someone as seemingly extroverted as herself would need to join Toastmasters. "Oh, John," she sighed. "I'd started this company. And after building it, suddenly, I had to lead it. I had to inspire a lot of people in a lot of faraway places to do their job well and to really, really care about what we do. And guess what? I wasn't great at it!" She laughed. "When it was time for me to give speeches and play the role, I'd get up to the front of the room. I'd thank everyone. And then I'd just feel like a total fraud. Like, 'Why did you ask me here?'"

Fields Rose traced her speech anxieties back to childhood. "I grew up with five older sisters," she said. "I'm sure they didn't mean to be harmful, but their nickname for me was 'Stupid.' When they asked me to do things for them, they'd say, 'Hey, Stupid.' It really affected me. So whenever I had to give speeches, I mean, I don't even know how I did it. All I could think about was, Oh my gosh, I'm stuttering. I'm pausing, I've said too many *er*'s—not the content of my presentation."

In 1979, Fields Rose joined Toastmasters in Salt Lake City, Utah. Over the next six years, she developed a fail-safe method for reducing speech anxiety. "It's called *research, John.*" And then, echoing Al Hoffman's explanation of how thinking through the other person's point of view alleviated his speech anxieties, she told me about the transformative power of learning to choose words for a speech.

"When I'm asked to do a presentation, I make time to visit with whoever I'm going to speak to. I learn what they care about, what they struggle with, and how they talk about it. Once I absorb that, then, instead of me going up there and babbling about *my* story, we're having something more like a dialogue because I'm actively referring to *their* world. I'm talking *to them.* And that feeling of being a fraud goes away."

Fields Rose had recently been invited to address the customer service department of a nationally known muffler company. The moment she agreed to the gig, her old self-doubts resurfaced. ("Mufflers?" she laughed, imitating her inner critic. "Come on, Debbi, that's kind of a stretch. You better stick to cookies.") Equipped now with a technique to dispel her anxieties, Fields Rose visited a handful of the company's franchises and hung out with the service staff. "I learned about their challenges. I learned about, oh gosh, ABS lights and OBD2 fuses and EVAP faults. You know what I'm saying?"

She paused. "All that stuff about speaking from the heart and making a connection? It just means making a bridge from your world to theirs. And for me, if I'm talking to muffler people, that starts by learning about ABS lights!"

———

"Speaking from the heart" was a phrase I'd bumped into since my early brushes with Toastmasters. It had sounded like sentimental, Dale Carnegie–era pabulum. As with other well-worn terms from the business self-help lexicon—*confidence, leadership, success,* and so on—I'd held it at arm's length for being trite without considering that it simply meant being authentic and clear.

Despite my professed goal of learning the "art of connection," I'd realized how resistant to the idea I remained—at least, with my fellow Toastmasters. The embarrassment of my first few speeches had been intense, causing me to wall myself off from my clubmates in self-defense. When they asked me basic questions about my childhood, family, or work, I found myself giving vaguer answers than I otherwise would have, parrying their interest by asking questions in return. I'd also been thrown off by the reticence of my fellow Midwesterners. Where New Yorkers are famously dramatic and self-involved, Midwesterners, at least the Minnesotans I know, tend to downplay their emotions (even the voluble ones). They seemed harder to get to know than the people I was used to. Did I really need to know them deeply? After all, I rationalized, in a mere three months, our family sabbatical would be over and we would be returning to New York. For all of these reasons, I hadn't really let my hair down in my club in a way that comported with my mission.

One night, after raising my hand to volunteer for Table Topics, I received the following topic: "If you could live for a day in someone else's body, whose would it be?"

The question caught me off guard. I'd never wanted to be anyone else. Stalling for time, trying to collect my thoughts,

I ran through a hastily assembled list of people I admired (President Obama, Bob Dylan, Tina Fey) and people whose bodies seem extraordinary (Jackie Chan, LeBron James). I rose from my seat slowly, hoping that by the time my body looked ready to speak, my mind would be right there with it.

LeBron seemed like a no-brainer. Compared to me—a five-foot-ten-inch sports incompetent who spends far too much time sitting at a desk—who would be more fun to inhabit? The moment before opening my mouth and beginning to speak, however, I realized: *Wait, this is stupid. Why not choose someone you care about and start from there?* Like any new parent, I really only cared about one subject: my son.

By now I'd embraced the special Toastmasters greeting, "Ladies and gentlemen, fellow Toastmasters, distinguished guests." I hadn't come to love the words; in fact, they still felt awkward and nerdy. But I'd realized that they launched my speeches to this particular audience more efficiently and directly than any other words.

> I've never really wanted to be anyone else but me, but now that you mention it, I've been looking a lot lately at my son, who, as of tonight, is ten weeks old. I hold him every evening from about ten P.M. to one A.M. while my partner catches up on sleep. It lets me spend a lot of time looking at him.
>
> I've never been especially afraid to die or get old. I've never had a big fascination with staying young forever. But I'm fascinated by the incredibly rapid changes taking place in his body from day to day. The other morning I calculated that, proportionate to his life span, one day for him is like two years for me. And every day, every week, he

changes tremendously. Yesterday, I noticed that dimples had appeared in his knees as he's fattening up. They hadn't been there a couple of days earlier. I noticed that sometimes, he grabs the fabric of my shirt in a little fist.

I imitated his tiny fist, grabbing my shirt, noticing, as I looked around the room, that for the first time since I'd joined, my Toastmasters seemed to be as happily, sincerely engaged with what I was saying as I was while saying it.

He couldn't do it a week ago. Three days ago, I was changing his diaper in front of the mirror. And I noticed that the way he looked at me was different. Before that, he couldn't figure out the whole mirror thing. It interested him, but he didn't seem to register any awareness whether it was him or me he was looking at. Suddenly, he did.

So there we were, looking at each other in the mirror, and I raised my head up and made my silly, cartoon high baby voice, sort of an "elevator going up" noise. Then I made an "elevator going down" noise from high to low and lowered my head down to his level. He followed me with his eyes. Now, all of this stuff, the voice and the elevator, the up and down stuff, we'd been doing for a couple of weeks. What was new was for him to watch it in the mirror. I repeated it two more times. And he got it! He followed me both ways with his eyes, getting really excited. Then broke into a big smile. And it was very, very clear: this was funny. It was our first joke.

Pausing to locate the next best words, and failing to find anything simpler, I continued:

There's something about the plasticity of his mind, this evolving cognitive ability—

No. Too wonky. Immediately, I sensed a slackening in the audience's engagement. Remembering my manual's instructions—use vivid language, don't use abstract concepts—I took another tack. "It's like there's this little spark inside of him," I said, "growing bigger and more intense, every day." Spontaneously, with the word "spark," I gestured with both hands, from my eyes outward, indicating imaginary rays of awareness. I continued, "He's just this little personality, growing and coming into this world."

Everyone in the room seemed to lean forward and soften in unison.

My gesture caused me, in turn, to soften as well. I paused, and suddenly I began to get emotional. I tried to catch myself, but by then the feelings had already played across my face, and everyone had seen them.

> As I said, I've never been fascinated by youth, or wanted to be someone else. But when I look at the dramatic changes happening in his body, I find it fascinating. What a wild, thrilling sensation that would be. So: If I could be in anyone's body for a day, it would be my son's.

For the first time in my onstage life, instead of putting on my public speaking mask and trying at all costs to avoid communicating anything personal, I'd half-accidentally done the opposite. I not only said what I meant, I made use of my newfound tool for enhancing my meaning. Emotionally, it felt like a breakthrough.

At the end of the meeting, when it came time for prizes,

I won a parchment certificate for Best Table Topic. To be fair, the club gives out several certificates each night, for best jokes, best speeches, and so on. In fact, it's kind of hard to *not* win prizes here and there. But I was exhilarated. I hadn't won the prize for Best Bullshitter, Best Panderer, or Best Imitation of a Guy Pretending to Be Sincere and Openhearted About His Kid. I'd connected.

5

THE POWER ZONE

n mid–September, I received an email from Gary Milter, the Vita Coco–loving software salesman:

Hey John!

My 30 seconds worth:

You are good at: putting together a good story; the most important part!

Need to work on: your delivery. Clear, consistent vocal tone—not too fast and don't drop off @ end of sentences. Make peace with gestures; you tend to go to clasped hand on wrist/hands in pockets mode. Think about bending your elbows and getting your hands more at chest level. Takes some practice, I know!

GREAT JOB—you are a fun addition to the club! Have a great weekend—

Gary

Milter's note cut to the heart of my vestigial paranoia about corrupting my "deeply authentic" self. Before I joined the club, thinking about myself too much or altering my "natural" behavior had seemed like a form of immorality, something between phoniness and pretentiousness. Honest, straightforward people, I believed, should shoot from the hip—even when they suck at it.

My first few exercises had taught me that feeling uncomfortable (because I was testing a new form of behavior) had nothing to do with behaving falsely. The pared-down speeches I'd delivered so far scarcely reflected my deepest thoughts and attitudes, but step by step, on a nonintellectual, look-people-in-the-eye and try-your-best-to-actually-say-what-you-mean-instead-of-faking-it level, the exercises were unquestionably encouraging a more genuine side of myself to emerge. All good, it seemed, until the moment Milter suggested that I think about bending my elbows. (What, and stop jamming my fists into my pockets?)

Margo Forster had taken me aside one night and urged me to read an online Toastmasters brochure called *Your Body Speaks,* offering tips about gesture and body movement:

> Stand straight but not rigid with your feet about six to 12 inches apart, and one slightly ahead of the other. Balance your weight evenly on the balls of your feet. Lean forward just a little. Your knees should be straight but not locked. Relax your shoulders, but don't let them droop. Keep your chest up and your stomach in.

I found the directions outlandish. I'd *just* managed to learn to stand in front of my group, remember my lines, and deliver them without falling to pieces. How could I be expected to assume the additional burden of worrying about the balls of my feet, the width of my stance, my knees, my shoulders and chest, all at once? Such feats of coordination seemed better suited to one of those old-school clowns who balanced spinning plates on sticks.

Thus it was that with great trepidation, I began working on my fifth Toastmasters exercise, "Your Body Speaks." My manual explained that I should select a topic that facilitated the use of body language, then learn to make my actions, both "in play" and at rest, appear smooth and natural. Instead of allowing my body to distract from my message, it explained, I should use stance, movement, gestures, facial expressions, and eye contact to express my message and to achieve my speech's purpose.

Fall, by now, had begun its graceful asphyxiation of summer. From my desk, I marveled at the circle of trees—orange, yellow, some still green—prettily outlining Lake Calhoun. The sailboats had gone, their navigators returned to office and school. The sky, unburdened by humidity, hovered lightly.

I decided to speak about how to ride a New York subway. Eager to avoid the mistake of my last speech, I took a few moments to reflect on the speech's purpose. It was fine to talk about New York or any other subject beyond the world of my Minnesota Toastmasters—as long as I fit the topic to their interests. Why not, I thought, construct the speech as a guide for tourists? "If you're ever planning on visiting New York, here is how to handle troublesome moments on the subway. . . ."

I organized the speech around three demonstrations of subway etiquette: How to avoid touching the center pole of a subway car with your fingers; how to force seated space-hoggers to make room for you; and how to exit the train when crowds on the platform are standing in your way.

As I practiced my moves, blocking out my physical gestures and movements, it all seemed simple and easy. But then I got to the harder, deeper stuff about how I was supposed to *act* and *seem*. My manual seemed intent on coaching me to the utmost neuron. "If you slouch your shoulders and fix your eyes on the floor, your audience thinks you're shy and weak." "If you repeatedly shift your weight from one foot to another, you appear uncomfortable and nervous." I understood that jamming my fists into my pockets wasn't good; it's distracting to an audience when a speaker physically radiates discomfort. But wasn't all this stuff about *seeming* this way or that just a form of "acting confident"? The emphasis on thinking so much about my appearance felt unseemly.

As always, when I felt threatened by my Toastmasters exercise, I took refuge in research. From the outset of my interest in speech, I'd imagined there must be reams of scientific insights on the subject. Indeed, when I looked online, I found scores of studies about the mental, chemical, and neurological processes of talking, hearing, listening, sympathizing, lying, memory retrieval, and so on that transpire during the process of communication. Many of these findings were fascinating, none more so than the portrait of the brain during speech production.

As mentioned earlier, the average American speaks 16,000 to 20,000 words per day. In the span of about 400 milliseconds, our memory retrieves each one from a data bank of 30,000 to 50,000 of the most common English vocabulary words, then arranges them into sentences averaging ten words apiece, evaluating, selecting, and composing along the way the most grammatically suitable combination from an astonishing 3,628,800 possibilities.

The simple act of saying, "Howdy, y'all!" requires careful choreography between some dozen different brain regions. A part of the temporal lobe known as Wernicke's area interprets the words we hear, then selects the words we wish to answer with. Broca's area, in the frontal cortex (just above and behind the left eye) anticipates the sounds we'll need to formulate them and assembles a sequentially ordered task list of nerve and motor firings required to make them. It sends the list to yet another brain region, known as the motor strip, which delegates the commands to a hundred-some orofacial and respiratory muscles—lungs, throat, jaw, palate, tongue, lips, teeth—producing as many as fifteen distinct, discrete sounds per second. Unlike the more conscious, artistic side of speech (which is to say, the subject of this book), for the average person the machinery of speech production is nearly failsafe, performing its tasks with an error rate calculated to be somewhere between 0.001 percent and 0.000059 percent—only one mistake every 17,000 words.

Science, I learned, had plenty to say about body movement. I'd dug up an fMRI experiment conducted by a group of Colgate University psychologists studying gesture and comprehension. They discovered that when speakers, for example, used words like "throw," "catch," or "wave" while making hand gestures (that is, using appropriately synced words and gestures) their listeners' brains comprehended their meaning faster than when they heard the same words unaccompanied by gestures. When speakers used those same words while gesturing with their *feet,* however (inappropriately synced words and gestures), their listeners' processing speed and comprehension rate dropped significantly, clouded by what scientists called "neural dissonance."

A University of Chicago psychologist named Susan Goldin-Meadow had worked for decades in the field of body movement, exploring "the intersection between gesture and meaning." Collaborating with linguists and cognitive psychologists, she'd conducted experiments using motion capture equipment to study how people demonstrate ideas. Over the course of several papers, she articulated the theory that words and gestures follow separate, parallel tracks. Words convey facts and events; gestures convey our attitudes and feelings about them. By establishing the contextual backdrop—irony, awe, humility, impatience, passion, and so forth—against which our words are meant to be interpreted and understood, wrote Goldin-Meadow, the information imparted through gesture is more than "a garnish we add to speech; it's often the very location of meaning."

But after browsing hundreds of such studies, many of which I found illuminating, I began to sense a kind of categorical limitation about them: They didn't seem to *go anywhere*. Science had developed imaginative ways to observe and describe the physical and biological processes of communication. It could offer compelling visuals depicting the frantic activity of an unskilled liar's mind flitting about from one brain region to another, assessing potential scenarios for deceiving a listener. It could sense, through analysis of vocal tones, whether a speaker was depressed or off their meds. It could count the number of times a speaker (or an email writer) used personal pronouns and posit with shocking confidence that people whose use of the word "I" comprises 6.5 percent or more of their total word count are often depressed or even suicidal. It could offer fascinating theoretical hypotheses about the workings of mirror neurons which (supposedly) drive our empathetic reactions to others' pain and suffering. What science could *not* do, however, was offer greater control over the processes it described.

Aristotle's *Ars Rhetorica* offers a single piece of advice about body movement, a prescription covering all aspects of delivery that he calls "correspondence to subject." "If we wish to be believed," he writes, "we neither speak casually about weighty matters nor solemnly about trivial ones." His point seems straightforward enough: If you're speaking about the death of a child, let your delivery reflect the gravity of your subject. Likewise, if you're talking about something funny, let your delivery reflect the levity of your words. Like every aspect of speech, wrote Aristotle, the underlying principle of using gesture in speech comes back to the audience. "Audiences," he continued, "believe speakers who behave as they do; when speakers behave inappropriately, their credibility is questioned—even when they speak the truth." The idea, I'd learn, would prove tremendously hard to absorb.

In August 2011, almost a year before I joined the organization, I'd gone to the Bally Hotel in Las Vegas to attend the Toastmasters World Championship of Public Speaking. I'd never seen a speech contest before and was, therefore, brand-new to Toastmasters' embrace of motivational, inspirational speaking styles and topics. Over the course of watching the two-day contest, I observed some two dozen speakers.

The first to take the stage was a dapper fifty-something African American man wearing a flashy double-breasted suit with a pink handkerchief sprouting elegantly from the breast pocket, delivering a speech about the power of perseverance. He looked and moved like a dancer, wheeling and prancing in a blatantly choreographed way, touching his fingertips to his heart to convey pain, tilting his head back and looking heavenward while pressing the back of the hand to his forehead to convey exhaustion. Describing the disappearance of his life savings after a failed investment, he exclaimed, "My little nest egg soon scrambled!"

I found every aspect of his presentation trite and over-the-top. I was bored by the message and turned off by pretty much every move he made to express himself. But even as I turned up my nose, I remained transfixed. I couldn't take my eyes off of him. This essentially schizophrenic reaction—of disdain and fascination—repeated itself throughout the day as successive contestants took the stage, dishing up equally histrionic, high-wattage homilies about the power of faith, the power to make a difference, the power of children, the power of listening with the heart, the power of experience, and last but never least, the importance of being in the moment.

As the day proceeded, my disapproval grew. None of what I was watching seemed connected to my fancy intellectual and cultural curiosities about language theory, the "art of connection," or my preoccupation with America's increasing social and political divisions. Driven by the vehemence of my own personal likes and dislikes, I failed to discern that the contestants hadn't flown to Vegas for the John Bowe Elevated Discourse Contest; they'd come to demonstrate a distinct set of skills before an experienced panel of Toastmasters judges evaluating them upon criteria having nothing to do with me. My inability to view their behavior on their terms, not mine, would ultimately prove an indictment of my own ignorance— and a principal stumbling block in my own quest to become a better speaker.

I'd never heard a single soul at Toastmasters mention the

word "rhetoric" or the ancient Greeks who'd invented it. But everything I would learn about public speaking, in and out of Toastmasters, went back to Aristotle's *Ars Rhetorica*. Whether we're championing our sincere beliefs, conning someone out of their fortune, or making everyday chitchat, there are three means, wrote Aristotle, by which we seek to persuade our listeners:

Logos—facts
Pathos—the emotions we stir up in our audience as we lay
    out our facts
Ethos—our character

Of these the most important—by a millionfold—is ethos: character.

In real life, "character" refers to our bona fide moral qualities—the stuff people know about us, our reputations, and so on. In public speaking, however, the term refers purely to how people *perceive* us. This includes our "genuine self" insofar as our audience knows who we are, but it also includes the degree of credibility we create through the competence with which we present ourselves and our information.

Suppose you're on a stage. You have a message. It's awesome, urgent, and 100 percent true. But is it clearly organized? Is it expressed with words and examples your audience can understand and relate to? Are you audible? Are you offering too much or too little detail or talking too fast or talking with an accent or wearing preposterous earrings or mentioning Harvard too many times or doing something slightly gross with your upper lip that distracts from the 100 percent true and urgent information you're trying to share? Are you pretty?

Do you have a weird haircut? Do you *not* have a weird haircut while speaking to an audience of people who mistrust speakers who don't have weird haircuts? If you have failed to adjust and align any of these stylistic aspects of your delivery to the needs and expectations of your audience—in other words, if you have failed to connect with them as well as you possibly can—do you really think they're capable of hearing your message with undivided attention? How well do you listen when you're talking to someone who has staggeringly bad breath? How well do you listen to someone who's shockingly good-looking?

You might think—as reasonable people do—that substance is (and should be) more important than style. You might think that it's "bad" if style trumps substance, or that only gullible, superficial people would ever fall for such a thing. Aristotle's point, to put it crudely, is: *too bad*. Regardless of our audience's intelligence or education, wrote Aristotle, "character is the controlling factor in persuasion." Aristotle complains, more than once in his treatise, that in a perfect world people would make decisions based on facts. The wisdom of the *Ars Rhetorica,* however, is in laying forth a prescription for dealing with the world as it is, not as we wish it were. And Aristotle's painful point is that being right, being smart, and having great facts won't carry the day when you're trying to reach people who are different from you.

Why do horrible, deceptive, blatantly awful politicians seem so often to win elections? Is it because voters are dumb? Or is it equally, to channel Aristotle, because nice, smart, thoughtful people—you there, reader—remain aloof to the imperative that we must meet people on their level, not our own, and speak in ways they can embrace and understand?

For the author of the *Ars Rhetorica,* the answer—and, in fact, the definition of what it means to be smart in the arena of public speaking—was dauntingly clear:

> Things that are true and things that are just have a natural tendency to prevail over their opposites, so that if the decisions of judges are not what they ought to be, the defeat must be due to the speakers themselves, and they must be blamed accordingly.

Translation: If your aims are genuinely good and true but you find yourself perpetually outmaneuvered by scoundrels, blaming the audience is a form of intellectual dishonesty. Being smart means winning the election.

Which brings us back to my reluctance to get my hands out of my pockets or to accept the reality that even the most authentic human being in the world must learn to use his or her body in ways that might not, at first, feel natural.

In the third week of September, the week before my speech, I had to fly to New York. By coincidence, I'd learned that a friend of a friend had become a professional speech coach working with "C-suite" executives from media and tech companies. His name was Joe Dolce. I shot him an email asking if he'd have an hour for me to discuss his thoughts on body movement.

We met at ABC Kitchen, an organic restaurant in Manhattan's Gramercy Park neighborhood. Dolce—fiftyish, wearing designer glasses and a suit with an open collar—shook my hand warmly and jumped right in.

"Telling people specifically how to move doesn't usually work," Dolce explained. "Not for most people." Sometimes, he said, yes, he'll direct an arm-drooper to keep his or her hands in what he called the "power zone" (between the navel and chest) or suggest a stage-cross at a specific moment to punctuate or enhance a story. Once, he remembered, he'd scripted a specific moment in a board presentation for a CEO to take a sip of water.

But generally, he said, body work begins in the head, not the body. "When you walk onto the stage," he asked, "where are you looking? At the left side of the audience? At the people in front? Okay, great. Now imagine taking the steps you're going to take as you enter the room. You're going to want to make eye contact. How slowly do you need to walk to do that? Keep feeling it out." He paused, gently pantomiming the action of walking toward a podium. "See what I mean?" Dolce asked. "It's not esoteric. It's very basic, practical stuff. You get yourself to the mic, look at your notes—or not—and do this with every step of your speech. If you're focusing on your content and your audience and visualizing how to be as clear as possible, you don't really need to think about, 'Oh, what should I be doing with my hands?'"

When I told him what my speech was about, he ran me through a series of questions I never would have thought to ask: "What train are you on? Was it raining before you boarded it? Are you carrying an umbrella? Where's everyone else around you?" Step by step, Dolce walked me through the motions of my speech, prompting me to visualize my imaginary circumstances and what my audience would see as they watched me. At almost every turn, he urged me to slow down and perform each gesture as fully as I would in real life.

As coffee was served, Dolce told me that the average TED speaker rehearses for over one hundred hours. "I've had clients ask, 'But doesn't that make it stale? What about spontaneity?' It's the opposite," Dolce explained. "Practice is what allows you to pay attention. And that's what public speaking really is: It's the art of paying attention. It's the art of not being boring." He paused. "People always try to complicate this. Especially the more highly placed, senior people. But it's not intellectual. It's not rational. It's not about thinking; it's about making an emotional connection."

When I returned home and practiced my speech the way Dolce had instructed, I overcame my hesitations about the exercise. I wasn't thinking anymore about acting this way or seeming that way. I was focusing on how to be clear. The next night at Toastmasters, after being introduced, I walked to the lectern, shoulders loose, physically relaxed, hands no longer thrust into my pockets. In the same way that thinking about the audience (instead of myself) had lessened my anxieties at every turn, thinking about *what the audience would be looking at* instead of thinking about *how I should move* proved easy to do and far more comfortable.

At the end of my subway tutorial, I shifted gears toward the homestretch, aiming to sign off with the customary conclusion, "Mr. Toastmaster, distinguished guests, fellow Toastmasters." I realized with a start, however, that the phrase wouldn't do this time. Normally, club members scheduled to give speeches do not volunteer for officer roles. By chance, however, the evening's appointed Toastmaster had called in sick, and I'd signed up for it. I was "Mr. Toastmaster." So when it came time to say "Mr. Toastmaster," I paused and pointed to myself while striking a silly, self-important pose, then continued, as everyone laughed, including me. It wasn't the most objectively funny line of the speech. On paper, I realize, it doesn't seem funny at all. It remained, however, the most spontaneous and memorable moment of the speech, precisely because it exposed more of "the real me" than anything I might say about riding the subway. Would this lighter-hearted, truer side of myself have ever emerged if I hadn't rehearsed my speech to death and gotten my fists out of my pockets? No way.

6

LETTING IT ALL HANG OUT

At 3:15 P.M. on March 29, 2009, David Moss found himself seated at the head of a long, ornately carved conference table facing a semicircle of thirty English bankers wearing high, starched collars. As if from another world, he heard a voice—his boss's—saying, "David, why don't you take it from here?" Moss felt himself rising to his feet, confronting the precise circumstance he'd dreaded his entire life.

Moss, forty-eight, a father of six, was the head systems designer for a prestigious Wall Street bank. He'd flown with his boss from New York to persuade the London office to adopt a $40 million foreign currency platform whose development he'd led. His boss, the smooth, socially adroit relationship manager, would normally have been the obvious choice to make the pitch, but knowing, as he did, the Brits' lack of enthusiasm both for new technologies and for Yankee brashness, he'd decided to let Moss lead the way with his low-flying technical brilliance. All Moss would have to do was explain how the system worked. The problem, unknown to anyone else in the room, was that Moss, along with three million other Americans, was a stutterer.

In the world of stuttering, Moss is what's known as a "covert," a stutterer who hides his affliction well enough to fool everyone around him. In childhood, he'd struggled with every syllable. After many years' frustration and therapy, he'd learned to pronounce words beginning with consonants. But no matter how hard he worked, words beginning with vowel sounds continued to thwart him. "And so," Moss explained, "I learned to fake it. To pause. To think ahead, sentence by sentence, getting rid of vowel words, dragging out my consonants in a way that allows me to start vowel words with them—whatever it took to get the job done." Moss's friends, colleagues, and even his own children had no idea he was a stutterer (he and his wife hid the fact from the children for fear it might make them anxious and exacerbate their own genetic predisposition to stutter).

Moss remembers staring mutely at the London bankers, entirely unable to open his mouth. "I started sweating," he recalls. "I felt my chest constrict. I couldn't breathe." At last, he ventured an old trick from speech therapy. "I started speaking like I was in the middle of a sentence, as if I were already talking. Sometimes it works." He sighed. "I think maybe five words came out. And then . . . that was it."

In a meltdown, he said, your mind goes back to that terrible place in childhood, a white-hot center of shame filled with memories of every previous humiliation. Every bully, every disgusted date. "I could literally see the letters and words I wanted to say, flying around in my head. I just couldn't get to them. I will never forget that day." Moss choked up. "I doubt anyone in the room forgot, either."

Moss returned from the London debacle newly resolved to overcome his stutter. For years, he'd seen flyers advertising his bank's private, in-house chapter of Toastmasters. He had ignored them—after all, why would a stutterer seek extra opportunities to speak in front of others? But in September 2011, upon the advice of a speech therapist, he decided to join the club, and at the very first meeting he took the radical step of what covert stutterers call "disclosing." He told his audience about his stutter.

Stuttering has long been attributed to acutely high levels of self-monitoring. Defined as the ability to observe ourselves and tailor our expressive behavior to accommodate social situations, self-monitoring levels vary widely among individuals.

Low self-monitors devote a less-than-average share of their consciousness to "fitting in" and getting along, coming across (depending on your point of view) as admirably un-self-conscious or socially difficult and uncompromising. At the extreme reaches of low self-monitoring we find sufferers of severe autism, whose insensitivity to social cues confines them to utter isolation.

High self-monitors, by contrast, are defined by their fluid, attentive responses to social cues. Generally perceived as "easy to get along with," they come across as skilled at going with the flow or, again, depending on your point of view, slightly insincere, perpetually hiding their true self behind a protean public persona. Studies have shown that high self-monitoring correlates with success in relationships and leadership positions. Except, of course, at the extreme end of the scale, where too much self-consciousness about performance causes stuttering.

Decades of scientific research have yet to produce a cure for stuttering. Throughout history, the most effective treatments have been decidedly unscientific remedies designed to trick, distract, or somehow induce stutterers to monitor themselves less, or at least to monitor themselves differently. Demosthenes, a fourth-century B.C. Athenian statesman and probably the most renowned orator of ancient times, overcame a debilitating stutter by practicing speeches with his mouth stuffed full of pebbles, rehearsing speeches while running up steep hills, and standing at the seashore shouting into the wind. Writer Henry James and *New York Times* critic John Russell, both stutterers in their native English, learned to jog their self-monitoring apparatus by switching to French. In the acclaimed 2010 film *The King's Speech,* King George VI, played by Colin Firth, is helped by speech therapist Lionel Logue (Geoffrey Rush) to cure a crippling stammer by singing, standing on his toes, and covering his ears while speaking to prevent him from hearing himself.

Moss, ironically, found treatment for his stutter in the precise aspect of public speaking that makes most new Toastmasters cringe—the constructed, artificial nature of prepared presentations that distinguishes them from "everyday talking." "When I wrote my first speech," he said, "I automatically got rid of all the vowel words that trip me up. When I went to deliver it, the shock wasn't how nerve-racking it was, but how amazing it felt to talk without all the scheming I usually do to navigate around my stutter."

As he advanced through the manual, learning to organize speeches, to choose his words and practice his gestures in advance, Moss felt increasingly liberated from the stresses of everyday speech, a process he likened to editing. "In normal life," he explained, "our minds are always going in a million directions. It's really hard to be present. When I prepare a speech, I get to pare my thoughts down to their essence and figure out who I want to be."

Since the onset of his stutter, Moss had viewed conversation as a threatening activity to be rushed through as quickly as possible. "Like most stutterers, I hated the sound of my voice. Silences completely freaked me out," he recalled. His evaluators in Toastmasters had coached him to slow down (the ideal speaking voice tends to be around 120 to 160 words a minute). "They told me it's actually good to have little pauses here and there so people can catch up. That's what allows people to get to know you." Moss laughed. The idea—of *letting* people get to know him through his voice—had never crossed his mind.

Moss's stutter isn't cured so much as it is in a state of remission; it surfaces now and then in rare moments of duress. He recalls no specific Hollywood moment of triumph over his malady; rather, he merely noticed the feeling when, for the first time in his life, he began to enjoy the act of speaking to other humans. "I was standing up there, giving a speech," he said (he doesn't recall which speech it was), "and I was making eye contact. And breathing. And pausing. And letting them hear my voice. I just felt overcome with a sense of connection." He began to tear up. "I'd hidden it for so long. So, to hear myself, and have everybody hearing and watching me, and have it be okay—I would describe it as a feeling of intense love. I know that sounds crazy, but I'm sure it's what drugs must feel like!"

I thought of Moss as I walked into my church office one morning in early October to begin working on my sixth exercise, "Vocal Variety." The instructions for the assignment read, "Choose a topic requiring you to vary your volume, pitch, tone, and rate of speaking to add meaning and liveliness to your message."

At the end of the last meeting, Lynn Reed had approached me. "John, you're funny. You want to participate in the Humorous Speech Contest?" The contest, she explained, would take place the following Wednesday. I thanked her, said I'd be happy to try, then asked if I could use the occasion to fulfill my manual exercise. I wanted to stay on schedule and get through my ten speeches by Christmas. Reed said that would be fine. "Just do the exercise in a funny way!"

So now, sitting at my desk, looking out the window, every leaf in sight fully brown, I decided to write a speech about the word "like"—specifically, about my loathing for its use (by me and everyone else in the world) not as a preposition, conjunction, verb, adverb, or simile, but as what linguists call a "discourse marker"—and what Toastmasters would call a "filler" word. I chose the topic for its relevance to my audience, but also because discussing its history would allow me to imitate a wide range of voices, from beatniks to Valley girls and, best of all, Caroline Kennedy, who in 2008 lost an easy shot at a U.S. Senate seat thanks to her overuse not of "like" but of another common discourse marker. The *New York Post* headline said it all: "Caroline Kennedy Repeats 'You Know' 142 Times in Interview."

Since joining the club, I'd struggled to find places to practice my speeches aloud that satisfied my admittedly ridiculous need for privacy. A quiet, secure room was not enough; I needed a quiet, secure room adjoined to *another* quiet, secure room. My manual had extolled the benefits of enlisting friends and family to watch one's practice, counseling that nothing sparks a speaker's desire to connect better than interacting with a live audience. Toastmaster and NBA All-Star defensive legend Mark Eaton told me in an interview that he sometimes paid his chiropractor to sit and listen to him. I wasn't quite there yet. My favorite place to practice remained the car. Alone and blissfully unobserved, as often as I could, I brought a printout of my speech, along with my laptop, parked next to one of Minneapolis's numerous lakes, and rehearsed my speeches several times over, writing, adjusting, then rehearsing again.

In the book *Simply Speaking: How to Communicate Your Ideas with Style, Substance, and Clarity,* Peggy Noonan, former speechwriter for President Ronald Reagan, offered the following advice: "When you falter, alter." The phrase describes perfectly how my practicing aloud helped call attention to word choices, phrasings, even ideas and opinions that might have worked on paper but sounded fussy, negative, hollow, or extraneous coming out of my mouth.

While ruminating about the exercise, I read a book by a famous English voice coach named Patsy Rodenburg. Our voice, she wrote, "is like a fingerprint," "an almost infallible form of identification." "As soon as we open our mouths . . . we are judged. Instant assumptions are made about . . . our intelligence, our background, class, race, our education, abilities, and ultimately our power." Daunted by the high stakes of exposure, wrote Rodenburg, most of us retreat into self-protective habits: We hunch, we slouch, taking shallow, guarded breaths while mumbling, clipping, and flattening our voices. These self-imposed limits confine us to crimped, baleful, stunted, inauthentic versions of ourselves, which in the end fool no one.

The perfect voice, felt Rodenburg, is neither beautiful nor

genteel, sexy nor stentorian, aims not for effect but for full, true, sincere expression of the speaker's personality. To this end, Rodenburg viewed her decades of work with actors, clerics, singers, and politicians as more than mere technical training but as a form of emotional and spiritual rehabilitation. "You have the right to speak," she wrote. "You have the right to breathe. You have the right to be yourself." I found her inspiring.

I, too, scarcely ever used my full expressive range—at least, not when it mattered. In lighthearted moments, I could easily, skillfully jump from low voices to high ones, from big ones to small ones, imitating accents from around the world. In speeches, however, or in serious, emotional everyday conversations, I tended, unconsciously, to throttle down my expressive capacity and speak in the flat, stunted vocal register Rodenburg described.

One day, while descending from my office to the church basement kitchen, where I'd stored my lunch, I was surprised to see that the church staff had left en masse. Perhaps they'd gone off-site for a meeting. Taking full and immediate advantage, I began to explore. I walked down the nave past the pews and, before I knew it, I was at the pulpit.

Like a kid in a canyon discovering his first echo, I began, timidly at first, to test the acoustics.

"Helloooo."

"Oooooo."

"Pop. Pop!"

"Yep-p-p. Yep-p-p-p."

"Op-p-p-p-p-pop-p-p-pop-p-p."

Moving on from *p* sounds, I found myself repeating the word "really."

"Reeeeeeelly?" (earnest, vaguely southeast Asian)

"Reeee-ully" (imperious Brit)

"Rilly! Rilly? Rilly!" (callow Valley girl)

My manual included several phrases to be recited with different tonalities: earnestly, sarcastically, simply, and with conviction:

I appreciate all you have done for me and I hope to return the favor someday.

If each of us does one kind thing for someone else every day, we could help make the world a better place to live in.

I repeated each sentence, cycling through a series of dramatic impersonations, from HAL, the pleasantly psychopathic computer from *2001: A Space Odyssey,* to Marilyn Monroe (circa "Happy Birthday, Mr. President") to Link from the *Legend of Zelda* videogame, then settled down to practice the exercise as myself.

I'd never paid much attention to my voice, but the giant room's acoustics allowed me to hear tonal components I'd never noticed before. I heard a pleasingly manly, resonant bass note that I liked. But I also noticed a lisp I'd never caught and a flat, Midwestern mushiness that struck me as appalling. My *t*'s in "better" sounded like *d*'s; my "live" sounded like "lev." "Better place to live" became "bedder place ta lev."

One of the revelations of my early days with Toastmasters had been how easy it was to fix certain kinds of speech problems. During the Ah Counter reports at meeting's end, when fellow clubmates might be cited for using three, four, seven, or more filler words, I found myself called out for using eleven during one meeting, seventeen in another. Within a month, though, the problem was gone. I'd only needed to become aware of it to develop the muscle for fixing it. The phenomenom repeated itself now as I spent thirty seconds repeating "bedder," forcing my lips, teeth, and tongue to pronounce the *d*'s like *t*'s. I probably looked like a donkey eating peanut butter as I struggled exaggeratedly to pronounce the sounds correctly. But after a dozen repetitions, my pronunciation improved tremendously.

Speaking. Correctly. And distinctly. At the pulpit. Enunciating. Each. Word. And its constituent tones. With precision. Quickly began to feel. Like a kind. Of rectitude. Like standing up straight, but in my thoughts. It didn't just affect my mouth; it affected the way I felt.

My evaluators had consistently criticized me for mumbling, for eating the ends of my sentences, and for generally poor enunciation. It hadn't occurred to me that speaking in a way people can't hear is rude. But as with my overuse of filler words, the mere awareness of the problem brought about a near-immediate correction. Slowing down, speaking clearly, and pronouncing my words with my full vocal capacity felt somehow relaxing, sensual, generous, and proper.

By now I'd studied scores of speeches and speakers from history: Lincoln, widely regarded as America's premier orator, whose 272-word Gettysburg Address is the worthy subject of an entire book by Garry Wills; Hitler (duly feared and loathed, but perhaps the only other orator in modern history whose vast political power and effect derived so singularly from his rhetorical capacities); JFK, RFK, Churchill, Helen Keller, environmental writer Rachel Carson, and former Texas governor Ann Richards (whose 1988 Democratic National Convention speech is a wonder to behold). I'd never tried to speak any of their lines before, but in recent weeks I'd become enthralled with a line from Martin Luther King, Jr.'s

1964 Nobel Prize acceptance speech: "I refuse to accept the view that mankind is so tragically bound to the starless midnight of racism and war that the bright daybreak of peace and brotherhood can never become a reality."

The words had struck me for their beauty, but also because they seemed composed in a register—of poetry and moral reach—that no longer existed. As I read the words out loud, phrase by phrase, it seemed impossible to imagine an audience today with the attention span and sophistication to take it all in. Were people only fifty-five years ago such superior listeners that they could easily comprehend complex sentences like this one?

In his 2008 book *The Anti-Intellectual Presidency: The Decline of Presidential Rhetoric from George Washington to George W. Bush,* political scientist Elvin T. Lim describes the devolution of presidential oratory over the last two centuries. Using a tool called the Flesch Readability Test, a formula computing the number of words per sentence and the average number of syllables per word, Lim indexed speeches to modern-day reading levels, rating *The New York Times* as typical college level; *Newsweek* at high school level; and comic books at fifth grade. Between 1789 and 2005, Lim determined, inaugural addresses had descended from a college reading level to about an eighth-grade one.

After repeating King's words several times, I felt exalted—lifted to a higher plane, not just of oratory but of courage and ambition. On a literal level, his words were perfectly simple—nothing an eighth grader wouldn't understand. What made them powerful was their rhetorical dimension. King's command of sound, rhythm, metaphor, and poetic word choice gave his statement immense moral and emotional depth.

I thought about what many ancient proponents of rhetoric believed, Cicero and Isocrates among them: that learning to speak in this higher register of meaning comprised a moral good in itself—an act of citizenship.

On the drive home from my workout in the church, I felt strangely elated. Isabel registered the lightness in my expression the moment I walked through the door. "What? Tell me!" she asked. I recapped my experience at the pulpit and asked her if she'd ever noticed my manly baritone (yes) or my lisp (also yes). I began to say, "We're so used to typing words and treating them as units of thought instead of sounds that come from our bodies . . ." and then trailed off, suddenly aware that I was meandering toward the spinning rainbow wheel of death. She looked at me expectantly. Instead of miring us both in conversational quicksand while I searched for the perfect words, I directed my attention to my newfound, even sensual pleasure in pronouncing words and continued, with ever-so-slightly exaggerated pronunciation, "It's astounding to see what comes to life when you communicate a bit more from your body and a bit less from just your brain."

I'd learned a new trick—as easy and helpful as memorizing one's introduction and conclusion. When in doubt about what to say, slow down and say the most obvious, easy thing that comes to mind and focus on pronouncing your words fully and clearly. If I'd expected Isabel to leap for joy, I should have known better. It's likely she didn't even notice. But getting out of my head and focusing more on my mouth while speaking made me feel more alert, alive, and connected to her.

"So, do I finally get to hear a speech?" she said.

High from my little triumph, I pulled out a chair for her,

turned on my laptop, grabbed a soup pot to serve as an impromptu lectern, set the stopwatch on my phone to time myself, and began:

Fellow Toastmasters and distinguished guests,

As Toastmasters, you're probably, like, painfully aware of, like, filler words and, like, crutch words and, like, slovenly, distracting, time-consuming, and generally unseemly and unfastidious word usages. I'm sure that you, as do I, get very sick of hearing them. Which is why I wish to discuss with you today the word which threatens to jeopardize the integrity of the English language: "like."

I do.

Not.

Like.

"Like."

Toggling between Samuel L. Jackson and various invented, fussbudgety characters, I milked the words "slovenly," "unseemly," and "unfastidious" for every potential drop of comic value while gauging Isabel's face to see what worked.

I traced the first documented use of "like," in the thirteenth century, through to *The Adventures of Huckleberry Finn,* when Huck's friend Ben Rogers says, "Now, that's something *like!*" I described a 1928 *New Yorker* magazine cartoon depicting two secretaries discussing a man's workspace. "What's he got—an awfice?" asks the first. "No," answers the second, "he's got like a loft." Isabel's face, alternately brightening with recognition or interest, then dimming with disengagement or incomprehension, served as running commentary on the success and failure of my efforts. Altering when faltering, as Noonan had suggested, I stopped, started, and repeated, adjusting words, lines, vocal tones, and timing—whatever seemed to work.

Over the course of our relationship, Isabel had often watched me read and mark documents in bed (and at my desk and in the car and on planes), then incorporate my notes at a laptop over countless hours. But she'd never seen the part of a writer's job that consists of continuously auditioning words and voices in his head, relentlessly evaluating the best way to express meaning.

It was embarrassing, intimate, and humbling all at once to practice in front of her, to show her different versions of "myself," and to admit to the very fact of needing to choose and rehearse which self to be. She herself had never had a moment's difficulty with public speaking; she'd never had to go through anything like this. But she'd gathered, by now, that my efforts were deadly serious, and transcended the silliness of the speech. I wasn't just trying to be funny; I was trying out ways to be myself in public.

I arrived at my meeting on the night of the Humorous Speech Contest to learn I'd be squaring off against Scotty Lindholm, a tan, sportily dressed retired insurance executive in his sixties who had belonged to Speakeasy for over a decade.

As we made our way through the Word of the Week, the Joke of the Week, and Table Topics, I caught him giving me a confident once-over. The hint of smugness, I suppose, struck a nerve and sparked my competitive impulses.

I'd been so preoccupied with preparing my speech, the thought of winning hadn't crossed my mind. Suddenly, it did. What would happen if I won? *What if I suddenly started kicking ass?* Toastmasters is composed of 15,900 clubs around the world, organized into 3,020 Areas, 310 Divisions, 78 Districts, and 8 Regions. In the event of victory, I'd automatically advance to the Area 93 Humorous Speech Contest. And then? Daydreaming, I found myself soaring, victorious, from my imminent contest to the heights of the Division, District, Regional competitions. With each step up the ladder, the crowds became larger. I couldn't quite tell what I was saying, but the audience laughed and smiled. I laughed and smiled. Whatever I was saying, it must have been great, because suddenly, with remarkably little strain, there I was, modestly, winsomely accepting the prize at the North American Humorous Speech Contest.

These thoughts took place in a five-second spasm, so fleeting that it would be overkill to call them delusions of grandeur (I'd also learn that there is no such thing as the North American Humorous Speech Contest). Ridiculous as they were, they offered a glimpse of something I couldn't deny. Beyond my intellectual curiosity about the history of rhetoric and what a re-embrace of speech training might do for America's lousy political discourse lay the simple desire to be known. To be clear. To measure up to whatever was inside me.

When we arrived at the contest portion of the meeting, Bobby Marino, serving as Sergeant at Arms, explained the rules. At the first utterance or gesture of our speeches, he'd start a timer. At four minutes and thirty seconds, he would hold up a green card. At six minutes, a yellow card. At seven minutes, a red card. Speeches shorter than four minutes and thirty seconds or longer than seven minutes and thirty seconds would be disqualified. Marino tossed a coin, slapped it heads-side-up on his palm, and said, "Yo, John. You're up."

From the introduction onward, my fellow Toastmasters

seemed amused. I described the first known usage of "like" as a discourse marker in the thirteenth century, its introduction into mass culture during the beatnik era, its explosion in popularity in 1982 with the song "Valley Girl" by Frank and Moon Zappa. I imitated Maynard G. Krebs, the beatnik character on *The Many Loves of Dobie Gillis* (played by Bob Denver, who would later take the starring role on *Gilligan's Island*), sang a line from "Valley Girl," then imitated Caroline Kennedy, all to consistent titters. My tone, pitch, and pacing went up and down, left and right, exactly as planned, and as I thanked my Toastmasters and concluded my talk, I knew that at the very least I hadn't screwed up.

Before I could heave a sigh of relief, Lindholm took the stage, composed in a way that signaled certain doom. Reminiscent of Dean Martin or some other '60s stage phenom, he looked as if he'd been born with a mic in one hand and a martini in the other. He greeted and thanked us, matter-of-factly assuming full control of our attention, and I wondered what bizarre sliver of my self-esteem had dared to fantasize about beating him. Around the room, my clubmates seemed to melt in unison, eyes widening, like puppies watching master open the treat bag—the treat, in this case, being the smooth ride of a good speech. And then Lindholm began to speak. "Today," he said, "I'm gonna talk about farting."

My clubmates shrank back in a pulse like a school of startled fish. Gordon Andersen, sitting next to me, visibly stiffened in his chair. I'd never in a meeting heard any kind of potty talk, off-color language, or swear words, not even "hell" or "damn." As Ralph C. Smedley, Toastmasters' founder, had admonished in his collected writing, entitled *Personally Speaking*, "The world is so well stocked with keen, clean fun that there is no excuse for playing in the mud to get a laugh."

Given Lindholm's many years in the club, his choice of topic was surprising.

Apparently unaware of the disapproval he'd aroused, Lindholm plowed ahead in a folksy, self-assured manner, using a variety of gestures and pleasing vocal variations, systematically laying out three distinct parables about flatulence, each offering a specific, well-defined point. At the end of each story, he reviewed its meaning, then transitioned to the next. He concluded by articulating the message of his speech: We are, therefore we fart.

We clapped for Lindholm as we'd clapped, presumably, for me, then Sharon Gifford, our evening's Toastmaster, took the lectern. After summarizing my speech and struggling to find euphemisms to describe Lindholm's, she instructed us to bow our heads and raise our hands for a vote. After a moment of silence, she bid us raise our heads. "Okay!" she said, beaming. "We have a clear winner."

It was me.

If I'd won by virtue of Lindholm's faux pas, it hardly mattered. I was thrilled.

At the end of the meeting, my evaluator, Anne Schiffer, praised my organization, commended me for my humor and choice of topic, noted my improved body language, then criticized me, in essence, for being somewhat insincere. "I appreciated the imitations," she said, "but I couldn't quite tell where you were, emotionally. What do you really think about 'like'?" She paused, then said: "I have a feeling you could be a really fun, dynamic speaker. But you gotta keep developing *your* style."

Her criticism was right on the mark. I'd sought to amuse my Toastmasters with funny voices and an antic manner, but hadn't thought to put anything of my genuine self into the speech. Did I really care about the proliferation of the word "like"? Kind of. But I also use the word as much as anyone else.

Since my second speech, when Gordon Andersen had suggested I approach my exercises like a musician practicing musical scales, I'd deliberately chosen easy, light topics. The advice had freed me up to focus on the technical lesson of each chapter, but it had also made it hard to practice "speaking from the heart." I'd joined the club, after all, not just to give random speeches but to express myself, specifically about subjects I care about. Schiffer's comments suggested it was time to step up my game.

One night, I accepted Andersen's invitation to visit his home and peruse the Speakeasy archives, a collection of photos he'd been curating for decades. (During this time he'd also served as writer, editor, and publisher of "Speakeasy News," an email newsletter he distributed every Sunday night around two A.M. The newsletter arrived every week without fail, impeccably edited, offering announcements for coming meetings and other Toastmaster events outside the club, like speech contests.)

I drove to his house, a two-story colonial painted in a shade he'd described as "good old-fashioned plain vanilla." Andersen greeted me without fanfare, then led me to the basement, where he'd already arranged two chairs before a half dozen boxes. These were the archives of old newsletters and photos—of Andersen, Hoffman, Forster, their spouses, and other Toastmasters I didn't recognize, quietly enjoying holiday parties and the Toastmasters annual lakeside summer picnics going back to the 1970s.

Surveying the smiles, vintage haircuts, and clothing styles, it was hard not to notice, *They're all white and, apparently, heterosexual!* Here were Robert Putnam's joiners, the now-mythical civic-minded mainstream of America, back when there was such a thing. For a moment I wondered whether these Americans had found it easier to be civic-minded back in the day—before diversity was part of the mix—because they were better, more sociable people (the Greatest Generation) or because, perhaps, in a society dominated by a narrow public identity (white, heterosexual, middle-class) the complexities of intermingling, at least for white, heterosexual, middle-class people or those inclined (or obliged) to interact with them, were simpler. Ironically, it's possible that in such a hierarchical social regime, where people outside the presiding paradigm were less free to "be themselves," fitting in with the herd seemed like an easier game.

I'd seen credible social-science findings suggesting that the more complex society becomes (specifically in terms of race, religion, and ethnicity), the harder it is to maintain social cohesion. If true, that might help explain why people no longer join clubs—it's just too hard to "be yourself" while interacting with so many different kinds of people. But it also seems like all the more reason for people to join a club like Toastmasters, which is fundamentally devoted to teaching the art of navigating difference. The organization was, in my experience, the least racist, most inclusive institution I'd ever seen.

Andersen had joined Speakeasy in 1981. His wife, Celia, now deceased, had joined in the early 1990s, as a charter member of a brand-new chapter called Super Speakers (associated with the SuperValu grocery chain, where she worked). Toastmasters had been a significant part of their lives.

Gordon had served in Korea and had seen crime and the misery of war from up close on many occasions. He'd worked most of his life in advertising and broadcasting. He currently belonged to three other social organizations besides Toast-masters, including Mensa, the international club for people with high IQs. He had lived a full life and retained a very active mind. He seemed to me to be an admirable model for living and aging gracefully.

As we chatted about his family, Andersen mentioned that in 1981, nine months after he'd joined the club, his twenty-year-old daughter, the youngest of three, had disappeared. She'd climbed aboard the back of a motorcycle belonging to a young man unknown to the family—and never returned. Presumably, she'd been murdered. "They never could pin it on anyone," he said. "It's the longest-running open matter in the history of the Saint Louis Park Police Department."

I was stunned. Andersen had told me this without emo-tion. Had he ever brought it up at Speakeasy? I asked. He shook his head. "There's stuff you just don't bring to your club." He paused. Here was the Nordic, Midwestern reti-cence I'd grown up with. In other parts of the country, for people of other ethnicities, the tragedy might have spawned an opera. Andersen had kept it under wraps.

As awkward as it felt to challenge his guidance—about avoiding controversial topics to keep the focus on technical form—I mentioned my desire to begin speaking about meat-ier, more reflective topics. If I avoided overtly divisive subject material, I asked, could I experiment with talking about pol-itics, social trends—stuff I really cared about?

Andersen shrugged encouragingly. "Sure. As long as you keep in mind: You're not just here to let it all hang out. You're there to give something to the audience. If you're talking about something funny, something serious—it's still the same techniques."

He'd risen and begun to close the photo boxes. As I followed him up the stairs, he continued, "People say charisma is something you have or you don't have. I disagree. If you really prepare, if you really do the work, that's when you stop worrying about yourself. By the time you speak, *whatever* you're talking about, you're giving them something. You're giving them respect."

7

FACTS ARE STUPID THINGS

My seventh Toastmasters exercise, "Research Your Facts," centered on the topic of data. My assignment: Write a speech using statistics, testimony, or other forms of verifiable evidence to support a thesis.

The manual explained how and where to do research (at the library, on the Internet, and so on), then offered a short list of guidelines for integrating facts within a speech: Use numbers and statistics sparingly; deploy a variety of styles and sources to add color and life to your presentation; whenever possible, translate numbers and abstract data into relatable everyday terms.

It didn't take long to settle on a topic: rising wealth inequality in America. I'd written about this (and related issues) for years. If I had a single, go-to, lightning-rod, fire-and-brimstone issue that I believed (correctly or not) exposed the root of America's ills, and about which I would love to proselytize, this was it: the increasingly concentrated distribution of wealth in the hands of the few.

At this point, I'd learned that what I used to think of as "speech writing" begins with sitting down to think about the audience. As Cicero had coached, *"Stilus optimus et praestantissimus dicendi effector ac magister,"* meaning, "The pen is the best and most efficient creator and master of speaking." Never mind what I thought, felt, or wanted to talk about, much less all the expressive ways I could state it. What was the best way to talk about it for this specific audience?

Burgeoning wealth disparity in America has been linked to a host of maladies: declining health outcomes (including rising infant mortality, rising maternal mortality, increased obesity and opiate addiction, and overall decreasing longevity) and decreasing economic, educational, and political opportunities for the majority of Americans. Which of these issues might my fellow Toastmasters care about the most? I decided to frame the matter in the most tangibly harrowing terms by emphasizing its impact on health and longevity. I titled the speech: "Wealth Inequality Will Kill You."

Now I needed to settle on a purpose. What did I want them to know or do as a result of my talk? Did I want my fellow Toastmasters to write their congressperson, to vote for a particular tax or healthcare policy, or to join me in a protest movement? None of these prescriptions seemed realistic. I wasn't working for a campaign or group involved with any of these potential solutions. In the end, I settled on a simple message: *I want my audience to agree with me that wealth inequality is the most urgent, important issue in America.*

At last I could grapple with the meat of the exercise. A ten-second Google search for "wealth inequality in America" yielded hundreds of sites oozing with statistics. I got immediately lost in minutiae. I realized I would need to block out a story of some kind, a context and plan for making my case. In the end, I decided to use evidence to make three specific points.

First, I'd explain what wealth inequality is, then show how it's gone up and down over the lifetime of our country. (The highest point of inequality, comparable to the present, was in the lead-up to the Great Depression.)

Second, I'd show how wealth is currently distributed in the United States. (The wealthiest 1 percent of families in the United States hold 40 percent of all wealth. The bottom 90 percent of families hold less than a quarter of all wealth.)

Finally, I'd list the many ill effects of wealth inequality, then zero in on life expectancy: between 1980 and 2010, life expectancy rose for the wealthiest 20 percent of Americans and declined for the poorest 20 percent of Americans. Rich women live 13.6 years longer than poor women.

The manual said I should make my information as relatable as possible. National statistics were fine, but it struck me that framing the information in local terms might be more relevant for my clubmates. A search for local statistics yielded the following treasure: the median annual family income in Edina, a wealthy suburb three miles away from Speakeasy, was over $96,000; the comparable median annual family income in North Minneapolis, three miles in the other direction: less than $22,000. Calculating proportionally against the longevity disparities I'd found on the national level, it seemed reasonable to predict that even within our club, some of us were going to live several years longer than others.

My manual had also advised me to vary the styles and sources of evidence. As a journalist, I knew the importance of being transparent about the provenance of my information.

For most of my life, the most trusted authorities tended to be U.S. government agencies, like the Department of Agriculture, the National Institutes of Health, the CIA, and the Census Bureau, as well as large global news organizations like Gallup and Reuters. It occurred to me now: In partisan, blog-driven, fake-news-driven, Internet-"informed" America, large swaths of the populace no longer trust such sources; data itself has become politicized. Citing facts, solid or not, obtained from *The New York Times* seemed likely to rankle the more conservative members of my club; citing facts, solid or not, obtained from Fox News seemed equally likely to turn off the more liberal members. Given the emotional power of facts' provenance, how might I vary my sources in a way that accommodated this new, post-objective landscape? Once again, I found my solution by turning to local sources of information. Many of the facts I needed had been published in articles by either the Minneapolis *Star Tribune* or the *St. Paul Pioneer Press.* Neither has a reputation of being more or less conservative than the other, but between the two, I'd managed to cite a variety of sources.

Juggling my facts to suit the political and hometown sensitivities of my audience had come easy, precisely because doing so jibed with everything I was learning about rhetoric. In the past, I would have approached the issue more rigidly. There's a right, there's a wrong; there's good data; there's bogus data. Persuading others to my way of thinking depended on proving my point—with sterling data. But as Aristotle had insisted, ethos (character), not logos (data), is the controlling factor in persuasion. The primary consideration for everything in a speech revolves around this idea—and no other. My idea of sterling data, then, could not be so fixed if connecting with people was more important to me than being right. The notion, which I'd just barely begun to absorb, seemed far away from modern sensibilities. But it also seemed of vital importance for navigating our current political moment.

In 2011, a Nobel Prize–winning professor of psychology and economics named Daniel Kahneman had published a bestseller titled *Thinking, Fast and Slow,* which explained with precision many ways in which our supposedly rational minds trip up, thanks to cognitive errors and perceptual biases with names like "the illusion of validity" and "base-rate neglect." Reading about the brain's loopy decision-making process made me wonder how we manage to cross the street. But it also whetted my appetite for more behavioral and cognitive research.

I searched online and found a professor of law and psychology at Yale Law School named Dan Kahan who had spent over a decade researching the following question: Why do reasonable people so often disagree about empirical facts? With scientific data available—about health, weather, crime, economics, politics, and so on—why is it so hard for people to settle upon commonsense, science-based solutions to common problems like gun violence, health insurance, or global warming?

In 2012, Kahan and a team of researchers began an experiment with over 1,500 volunteers. After surveying their subjects' political beliefs and testing their basic math and science literacy skills, they weeded out the volunteers lacking science- and math-based problem-solving skills (approximately 20 percent of the total). Those remaining were asked to consider a series of science-based public policy issues.

When asked to evaluate ideologically neutral issues like the effectiveness of antibiotics or the degree to which alcohol affects people's ability to drive, the subjects proved highly capable of reaching logical conclusions. When it came to heavily politicized issues, however, like gun control or climate change, the subjects' ability to evaluate straightforward factual information decreased precipitously.

Liberals were terrible at evaluating evidence concluding that certain types of gun control measures have little to no effect on reducing crime. Conservatives were equally abysmal at assessing scientific findings proving climate change is a growing danger. When data posed no threat to subjects' political beliefs, they proved adept at using it to make sound, objective decisions, but when it did, common sense went out the window. The more partisan the subjects, the harder it became for them to assay evidence that ran counter to their beliefs.

Kahan devised a theory he calls "identity-protective cognition," suggesting that when forced to choose between factual truth and group identity, most people choose the latter. "Individuals," he concluded, "subconsciously resist factual information that threatens their defining values."

Kahan's conclusions echo findings by political scientists and researchers working in the field of evolutionary psychology. For decades, political scientists have noticed, for example, that an improbably high number of Democrats (compared to the general population) incorrectly believe that inflation increased during President Reagan's presidency (it decreased). Republicans believe, incorrectly (in similarly improbable numbers), that the U.S. budget deficit increased during the Clinton and Obama presidencies (it decreased). Time and again, precisely echoing Kahan's findings, scientists have documented subjects' tendency to resist "logical" conclusions that prove to be ideologically inconvenient. Ironically, the more highly educated subjects reported themselves to be—they'd read or watched more news or otherwise accumulated more knowledge—the more often they answered *incorrectly* than their less-well-educated peers.

Kahan admitted that his findings were not what he'd hoped for. After years of experiments, he said, "I find it really demoralizing, but I think some people just view empirical evidence as a kind of device."

For the Greeks, of course, the idea that facts don't win arguments came as no surprise. The problem wasn't that people are dumb, irrational, or even superficial, as I'd formerly assumed. We've simply evolved—as a species—in a different way than I'd imagined.

As Jonathan Haidt, a professor of psychology at NYU, has claimed in his book *The Righteous Mind,* this tendency toward irrational decision-making makes sense in the context of evolutionary psychology. Once upon a time, our primate forebears learned that groups have a better chance of survival than those who travel solo. Over time, as bigger groups of primates prevailed over smaller ones, traits that foster group cohesion won out over the ability to reason. "Once group loyalties are engaged," Haidt says, "you can't change people's mind by refuting their arguments. Thinking is mostly just rationalization." We are, Haidt concludes, for the most part designed to be team players, not judicious evaluators of evidence.

Since its invention in the early days of democracy, the discipline of rhetoric spawned a bitter controversy: Was it good or evil?

For its proponents, it was good because it provided an educational foundation for teaching the average citizen to find their voice and engage more meaningfully in social and public life. For society as a whole, it was good because in a political system essentially powered by untamed free speech, shared knowledge of rhetorical theory and practice served as the indispensable means for grappling with arguments based on opinion, passion, belief, and personality; for seeing through demagoguery and what we would today call fake news.

And yet the idea that facts can—and must—be artfully framed to succeed in the marketplace of ideas has always aroused suspicion. Why should truth need help? For many, the study of persuasion seemed perilously synonymous with the study of bullshit. This distrust of rhetoric no doubt helped lead to its gradual decline as a force in society.

The causes for rhetoric's demise include the rise and dominance of the Christian Church (with its insistence that the Bible is the only source of truth and its tendency to disfavor the free flow of debate) and the invention of the printing press, which deemphasized such human, performative components of persuasion as gesture and voice, with their capacity to charm, manipulate, and deceive. The nail in rhetoric's coffin, however, was the dawn of the Enlightenment and the spread of the scientific method. Reason and science offered demonstrable proofs rather than "mere" persuasion. Both science and the printed page allowed facts to speak—or at least *seem* to speak—for themselves, freed from rhetorical spin.

By 1690, in his *Essay Concerning Human Understanding,* John Locke would assert that the tropes of rhetoric "are for nothing else but to insinuate wrong ideas, move the passions, and thereby mislead the judgment." Useful as such parlor niceties might be for "harangues and popular addresses," for *serious* communication, where "truth and knowledge are concerned," they "cannot but be thought a great fault, either of the language or person that makes use of them."

In the 1740s, Adam Smith would dismiss rhetoric as "a

silly set of books." In 1819, the Harvard literary scholar Edward Channing would describe its study as antiquated and bothersome: "We have now many other and more quiet ways of forming and expressing public sentiment than public discussion in popular assemblies."

By the 1800s, rhetoric, first among the liberal arts since their very invention, had been downgraded, stripped of its mission to navigate the realm of the irrational, then splintered into narrower fields of study: debate, elocution, philology, composition, declamation—all useful individually, but lacking the profundity of their mother discipline.

And, of course, the rest is history. Except it's not. Science is debated. Science is ignored. In our current political and globalized era, consensus about what is true or not true is subject—as it ever was—to debate. At a minimum, we have a hard time talking to people who don't know as much as we do. We feel this frustration in our everyday lives. We worry about the post-factual universe that's emerging. As our worries about fake news reach fever pitch, perhaps rhetoric might be the cure.

I'll skip the blow-by-blow description of my speech. As my evaluator, Laura Betz, the Chinese PhD student, would offer, "You did pretty good. Well-prepared. Good focus, organization. You followed the direction to use data appropriately. But your delivery was maybe . . ." She paused, then said, delicately, "What do you believe? Why do you care about this subject? You need to show your heart. Make us care more."

Once again, I realized, I'd learned an awful lot—while missing the obvious lesson of the exercise. Audiences care more about speakers' emotions, beliefs, and personalities than they do about the facts. As President Ronald Reagan, a.k.a. the Great Communicator, once said, "Facts are stupid things."

Reagan, of all people, knew well of what he spoke. It's hard to find a finer demonstration of his point than the moment, during the third debate of the 1980 election season, where he famously overcame former president Jimmy Carter. During a heated discussion of healthcare policy, Carter, attempting to attack Reagan's voting record as governor of California and accusing Reagan of being insensitive to the needs of the common people, had gotten bogged down in a data-heavy tirade. As Carter's focus on the audience wavered, Reagan, sensing the audience's fatigue with tiresome facts and specifics, grinned and began looking back and forth from the audience to his opponent, all but mocking his wonky earnestness. At the end of Carter's exertions, Reagan smiled genially and sighed, "There you go again." Carter had tried to use facts to show his concern for the American people. Reagan won the debate by focusing unwaveringly on the American people themselves. The moment proved a turning point in the election—which Reagan handily won.

By mid-October, the Byerly's parking lot had ceased to offer transcendent sunsets. The days had gotten short and dark, and local attentions had shifted toward Halloween and election season. My lesson about emphasizing beliefs and feelings over logic and facts would be on display during the first of three televised debates between President Obama and former Massachusetts governor Mitt Romney. Romney's momentum going into the match had been damaged by a recording catching the former hedge-fund manager quipping to a group of wealthy donors that 47 percent of Americans don't pay taxes.

Obama, a reliably powerful orator since his days as a junior senator, was expected to handily carry the match. Romney's debate coaches (I later learned) had prepared him to bait Obama with glib, biased, slanted statements of facts. The tactic played hard with Obama's professorial instincts, leaving the president sputtering in rebuttal, looking sour and petulant for much of the evening, and allowing Romney to run off with the contest. In the post-debate commentary on CNN, former Democratic campaign strategist and political pundit James Carville rued Obama's performance. "I had one overwhelming impression," Carville said. "It looked like Romney wanted to be there and President Obama didn't want to be there."

Byerly's management had requisitioned our meeting room to use as storage space for the upcoming Thanksgiving and Christmas holidays, leaving us to convene in a second-floor staff cafeteria space deep in the bowels of the grocery store. Meetings had taken on a slightly odd feel, as store employees traipsed in and out on their breaks, eating meals or sitting to gaze blankly at college football playing silently on a widescreen TV five steps from where we sat.

One night, Hanna Turnquist, the IT project manager who'd explained to me how Toastmasters was making her a better person, took the lectern to preside over Table Topics. Her theme: Halloween. She assigned Alex Čapek to tell us which type of monster he found scariest (vampires). Lynn Reed fondly discussed the days of yore when parents dispensed brownies and fruit; Anne Schiffer talked about the greatest fright of her life (a train derailment). Antonia Grefa was assigned to talk about "the meanest trick she'd ever played on Halloween." She graciously explained that kids in her home country didn't typically roam around at night committing damage to property lest they be shot by the military police. At last came my turn. "John," said Turnquist, "every year, at Halloween, the news carries stories about kids getting poisoned or receiving candy with razor blades in it. What should be done about food safety on Halloween?"

A friend had told me a story about a Halloween parade he'd seen in Provo, Utah, where several kids trick-or-treating together began throwing up. They hadn't been poisoned, he said; instead, they'd received an average haul of six pounds of candy each, way too much, apparently, to resist. The story combined with a report I'd seen finding that Halloween night is one of the three busiest nights of the year for hospital emergency rooms. I wove these facts together with a healthy admixture of bluster and commenced to deliver the opinion that Halloween is a menace. Do we, as adults, eat food from the hands of strangers? Not generally. Should we be allowing our children to eat food from the hands of strangers? Not on my watch. Should we be allowing children to eat so much sugar? I suggested not. Why in the world, I demanded, do we celebrate this holiday? With remarkable momentum and force, at least for me, I offered my conclusion: "Halloween should be banned, the sooner the better."

I'd never taken such a strong public stand before—on anything. The fact that my position wasn't really my honest viewpoint felt like a step backward. Apparently, my fellow Toastmasters hadn't cared that I'd performed something of a parody. At the end of the meeting, for the third time in my brief Toastmasters career, I received the parchment certificate for Best Table Topic. With three more speeches to go, I hoped, maybe I'd learn to be eloquent and honest at the same time.

8

SEEING IS BELIEVING

One night in early November, Gordon Andersen, serving as the evening's Toastmaster, introduced our next speaker, Antonia Grefa, the Speakeasy member from Ecuador. Grefa, a tall woman with astonishingly wide eyes and long, dark hair, would deliver her eighth manual exercise, "Get Comfortable with Visual Aids," a speech she'd titled "Space Is Big." I was especially eager to watch her perform because I'd soon be grappling with the same exercise.

Our eyes shifted to Grefa as she rose from her chair, strode halfway to the lectern, stopped abruptly, wheeled around in place, returned to her seat, and began rummaging through her purse. I took a sharp breath and prayed she wasn't having a panic attack. My reaction demonstrated the stark tension underlying every Toastmasters meeting. By signing up to learn how to "be ourselves" and submitting our performances to be graded (literally, by the Evaluator), it often felt like our personalities and even our very souls were constantly on the line. The old-timers, perhaps, were exempt from risk by dint of their long experience, but the rest of us seemed vulnerable, triggered by even the slightest stumble, to the terrors of a psychic wipeout.

I'd witnessed two indelibly painful moments during my time with Toastmasters. In August, a spectacular meltdown featured a timorous web designer I'll call Ray. Ray showed up week after week with the lower third of his face all but obscured by a large, brushy mustache. The upper third, including his eyes, was nearly blocked from view by a greasy baseball cap with an oversized brim. I'd spent two hours a week with Ray for four months. I'd barely seen his face, and had never once spoken with him.

Ray's misadventure—okay, let's call it a catastrophe—befell him during the very same visual-aids speech Antonia Grefa was to deliver tonight. The Toastmaster, Alex Čapek, had introduced him. Jen Shepard, the Sergeant at Arms, had started the timer. But where typically a speaker would take the lectern, greet us, and begin his or her speech, Ray paused to hover at a table several feet away from the lectern to fuss with what appeared to be a cluster of folded papers. As Čapek waited at the lectern, Ray dawdled, giving us his back for a full minute and a half. When at last he took the lectern and graced us with the third of his face we could see, he proceeded to violate a cardinal rule of every public speaking teacher in history: He began to apologize.

> Hey. Kinda frustratin' there. These are, uh—I think I was prolly—well, what I shoulda done there I guess was get the vellum-weight paper. And this is just like index-card stock.

So they don't stand up. Anyways, sorry for the delay an' all that.

Adjusting his hat and scratching his mustache, Ray looked down, down, and only down at the lectern, assiduously avoiding our gaze. Not a single member of the audience had the slightest idea what the hell he was talking about. At last he began to explain:

Yep. Anyways. So, well, the idea was, these are, ah, greetin' cards. And so what I'm—well the idea, the original idea here, is to show different ways to make your own greetin' cards.

Having at last informed us of the object of his speech, Ray returned to his prop table and, for all intents and purposes, stopped speaking. His focus devolved toward a greeting card, a folded piece of paper that seemed not to be standing properly. After one, two, three attempts to fix it, each of which seemed only to topple its neighbors, Ray began scratching his jaw again, muttering, "Hold on. Hold on. Come on, man!" A different speaker might have surrendered, opting to leave the cards alone, return to the lectern, and move on with the speech. Ray was not that speaker. His speech had degenerated into a battle between man and props. The props were winning.

At some point I realized Ray had slipped through a crack in the time-space-social-anxiety continuum, then tumbled abjectly into the full-on shame spiral of a Public Speaking Meltdown. He spent two, maybe three more minutes at the table with his back to us, muttering, apparently hoping that if only he held on long enough, kindly aliens would teleport him from his present coordinates to a galaxy beyond the Byerly's community room. If memory serves, there was no end to the speech, no conclusion. Ray simply trailed off, leaving the reproach of his infinite befuddlement to echo in my memory like the ceaseless, plaintive roar of the ocean in a conch. Or something.

The second public meltdown took place a few weeks earlier, when a smart, painfully shy teacher from Wisconsin suffered an attack of speech anxiety such as I'd never witnessed in my life. She'd risen to make a brief announcement regarding a routine matter of club administration, then gotten gummed up in her delivery. After forcing herself once, then again, to repeat herself with exaggerated clarity and deliberateness to get the words out, she finished. It happened so fast it's hard to imagine anyone really noticed. But as she sat down, I could tell she was extremely upset.

I'd always assumed that people blush in more or less the same way, with a bloom of fuchsia diffusing from the center of the cheek. In the teacher's case, the blush rose from the bottom of her neck in a wine-dark stripe ascending with the mechanical steadiness of an elevator to her chin and jaw, eventually staining her entire face an angry, deep shade of purple. It seemed she could feel the heat of it, because a couple of minutes later she rose from her chair and nearly ran to the bathroom. She returned to her seat, glowing with undiminished intensity, remained seated—looking agonized—for another three minutes, then bolted from the room and never returned.

Luckily for the club, Grefa's aborted march to the lectern portended no such meltdown. She'd simply wanted to retrieve a bottle of water from her bag before speaking. She continued to the front of the room, fixed us with a look, cleared her throat, raised her hand, and directed our gaze to a chickpea held between her fingers.

"This," she announced with gravitas, "is Earth."

Commanding our full attention, she circled the room, extending her fingers and holding the chickpea for each of us to examine. Returning to the lectern, she next retrieved a soccer ball, then held it aloft, and continued:

"This . . . is the sun."

She crossed the room, placed the ball on the table before Margo Forster, and resumed her place at the lectern.

Pointing to the garbanzo bean, then the soccer ball, she looked around the room at each of us and asked, "Now, if this is the Earth, and that's the sun, where do you think the next closest star is?"

She paused.

The closest star to the sun is Alpha Centauri. If you want to imagine where that is in relation to our sun, you would have to leave this room, pass the checkout counters, walk past the freezer section, past the dairy section, past the fruits and vegetables, all the way to the back of the store. And then? You'd have to walk out the door and keep going . . . all the way to Spain. Because that's how far—on this miniature scale—Alpha Centauri is from the sun.

Eyebrows shot up around the room, registering genuine surprise, prompting Grefa to respond with a quick smile and the facial equivalent of a curtsy. "That's my point. Fellow Toastmasters, honored guests, my topic today is the vastness of space. Space . . . is BIG."

Grefa's visual trick was so dazzling, I experienced a little rush. It was every bit as sensational as an expensive special effect in a movie.

I'd volunteered to serve as the meeting's Evaluator, so at the end of the evening, when it was time to give my report, I rose from my chair, walked to the lectern, and switched places with Gordon Andersen. This morsel of stage business, which I'd never once considered before joining Toastmasters, offered, I realized, a perfect window into the workings of public speaking. Prior to joining the club, I'd assumed it to be something a reasonable person shouldn't waste time thinking about. My approach—call it the Bowe method—consisted of winging it. Never mind that every time I took the lectern, my ignorance of how to do so properly resulted in the awkwardness that ensues when two passersby facing off on a sidewalk can't decide which way to steer.

The proper way to approach the lectern, I'd learned, has the approacher arrive as the speaker (at the lectern) finishes introducing them. The approacher pauses briefly, some eighteen inches from the speaker, as the speaker turns to face them. The two shake hands. The speaker at the lectern backs up, then departs as the approacher takes the lectern. Of paramount concern is—surprise—the audience, whose attention is maintained through the avoidance of clownish fumbling.

In a world with melting polar ice caps, a would-be orator might be forgiven for asking: *Who cares?* I'd realized, however, that if you happen to be the awesome, amazing person with the solution to melting polar ice caps, you'll have an easier time being taken seriously if people's first impression of you isn't a feeling of annoyance. Just as importantly, you'll have an easier time *feeling* like an awesome, amazing proposer of solutions to the problem of melting polar ice caps if your brain is filled with thoughts about your audience and your message instead of thoughts of self-recrimination, not to mention cortisone, adrenaline, and the myriad chemicals that flood our brains when we're anxious.

Having expertly taken my place at the lectern and greeted my fellow Toastmasters, I proceeded to evaluate Grefa's speech according to a checklist of criteria that appeared in my manual at the end of the exercise. Appropriate body language? Yes! Did the speaker turn her back to us? No! Did the speaker use varied forms of visual aids? Yes! Did the speaker choose appropriate words and use good research? Yes! I congratulated her on her effort, then carefully switched places with the Ah Counter.

After running the idea past Gordon Andersen, I'd decided to redo my speech about wealth inequality—this time using visual aids and foregrounding my beliefs and personal feelings about the subject.

The manual offered a straightforward list of principles for using visual aids: Keep them simple; show them just before you explain them; vary them in color and texture; make sure they're legible; and most important, never allow them to interrupt your eye contact with your audience. Inspired by Grefa, I decided to steer away from passive visual aids like slides and PowerPoint and to develop instead low-tech materials like hers that would keep me physically busy.

My mom had left town to visit friends in Arizona. I jumped at the chance to work in her apartment. Besides being closer to home and bigger than my garret office in the church, it also promised to be better endowed than our rented apartment with the everyday household materials I'd need for crafting visual aids. Indeed, as I poked around in the cabinets,

I found supplies of string, construction paper, tape, Post-it notes, and a stack of moldering game boards, apparently hoarded since my siblings and I were children.

Resisting the urge to jump in immediately and start playing with the materials, I forced myself to review my speech basics. Had my audience changed? No. Did I need to reconsider anything about them I'd previously overlooked? No. Had my purpose changed? Even as I asked the question, an internal hesitation seemed to register. How could I know the purpose of the speech before locating my personal connection to the topic?

I'd cared about wealth inequality for a very long time. I certainly had lots of *thoughts* about it. It was bad. It was harmful. It was unjust. But if you asked me what my *feelings* were regarding this subject I supposedly cared so much about, I would have drawn a blank. How had wealth inequality affected me, personally?

In the quasi-Scandinavian, heavily egalitarian Minnesota of my childhood, class issues had remained in the background. My public school mates included wealthy kids from the mansions along Lake Minnetonka, middle-class kids like me from a half dozen subdivisions, and poorer kids from the downtown area of our small town. No one seemed to notice, care, or talk about our differences. As a housepainter in both high school and college, I'd worked for some incredibly affluent homeowners. They'd always treated me like a friend or neighbor.

Only after moving to New York after college did I begin meeting people who wore their class unabashedly. I'll never forget the comment made by the thirty-something marketing executive whose SoHo loft I'd been hired to paint. I was high up on a stepladder, reaching unsteadily to paint the tippy-top of a skylight, when she asked, "John? Are you insured?" *How kind,* I thought. *She's inquiring about my well-being!* But then she continued, "Because if you fall and break my Pace Collection furniture, you're *never* going to be able to pay for it." A year later, when I started graduate school, I met a student who thought nothing of taking a taxi three blocks to the student grocery store.

If New Yorkers seemed to advertise their class more nakedly than I was used to seeing, it seemed, at least to me, more amusing than injurious. I'd chosen a speculative career in the arts. Money simply wasn't my priority. What could I say? I was above it all—a free spirit. Fifteen years later, after attending graduate school, chalking up $110,000 debt, then struggling to repay it (along with New York City rent and healthcare) on a freelance journalist's income, my spirit had become less blithe; I'd begun to feel poor in a middle-class country that seemed suddenly to become poor alongside me. But even then, the issue of wealth inequality felt impersonal. If America had begun to feel less civil, less neighborly, less generous, more insecure, threatened, and competitive, and harder to get by in than it formerly had been, the issue still seemed more macro than micro. These changes had happened to everyone, not just to me.

Only with my son's birth had the issue finally become personal. When I contemplated the economic and social factors conspiring to thrust him into a tensely competitive, mentally and physically unhealthy and unfun world, I grew white-knuckled with anxiety and even shame: How would I, how could I, protect him from a horrible future? Here, at last, was a meaningful vernacular for my speech, for what, if not widespread shame and anxiety, are the truest hallmarks of wealth inequality? Had anyone in the room not experienced intense stress about money and the future? I decided to title the speech, "Wealth Inequality Is Making Us Nuts."

My story would begin with a brief review of the previous speech, laying out the history and effects of skyrocketing wealth inequality. I'd describe the current landscape of increased healthcare and education costs and the decrease in well-paying jobs, explaining how these factors had narrowed access to what we once called middle-class life. I'd chart the rise of mental health issues and drastically increased drug usage, both legal and illegal, among vast numbers of Americans. Finally, I'd zero in on the reality that these issues were undoubtedly already affecting my clubmates and would increasingly swamp their loved ones' chances for a well-lived life.

Monopoly money seemed like an appropriate visual aid for describing the dwindling access to middle-class perks. After practicing more than a dozen times, rehashing and simplifying my statistical analysis, I devised a way to explain the economic and social facts that would allow me to walk around the room and hand out fifteen hundred dollars to everyone in attendance (just as every player receives at the beginning of a game of Monopoly), then go around the room again and snatch it all back, redepositing it in the hands of three participants. Here, I'd explain, was the new reality in America. In the very near future, only one in four of us will be able to afford what used to be taken for granted as "middle-class life."

After several experiments, I found a way to use Post-it notes to illustrate the rising incidence of mental illness and drug use. Over a large cardboard placard marked *1974* I'd place seven Post-it notes, and over a similar placard reading *2012* I'd place thirty-one. Meanwhile I would explain, eyes on the audience, that the Post-it notes represented the number of Americans per hundred diagnosed, two generations ago and now, with depression, anxiety, ADHD, or other mental and behavioral illnesses—or taking prescription drugs or, worse, illegal opiates.

As a final visual demonstration, I'd ask the audience members to raise their hands if they had kids, then ask everyone else: Do you have siblings who have kids? By now, I assumed, most of the hands in the room would be up in the air. At this point, I'd raise my own hand, include myself among their number, and explain that at the currently rising rate of anxiety, drug addiction, and so forth, exactly half of us would be dealing someday with kids facing the maladies I'd depicted on the wall. Who among us would have to confront the mental health effects of rising wealth inequality?

The speech was hardly upbeat, but after I'd spent hours devising and practicing with my DIY visual aids, the investment allowed me to waltz through my presentation without a hitch. Their smooth functioning gave me a boost of clarity, certainty, and charisma I hadn't expected.

Justly or not, I realized, visual aids serve as a kind of evidence, demonstrating probability with equal or greater force than logic. The best example I could think of was the famous "glove moment" from the 1995 murder trial of O. J. Simpson. The prosecution's case against Simpson enjoyed an overwhelming degree of scientific evidence against the defendant. But as the trial wore on, the credibility of the Los Angeles Police Department was severely impugned by admissions of blatant racism. The case, more obviously than most, came down to credibility and impressions versus facts.

After a long, painstaking, but virtually airtight DNA analysis linking Simpson to blood found at the murder site, prosecutor Chris Darden moved to have O.J. try on an expensive, extra-large men's leather glove that had also been found at the crime scene, covered with blood. The prosecution had repeatedly called jurors' attention to the glove, creating a keen sense of drama leading up to the moment. In retrospect, it's inexplicable that Darden failed to consider the risks of improvising any form of testimony unrehearsed. Simpson, wearing a rubber liner (as required by law, so as not to contaminate evidence), struggled theatrically while trying on the glove, aiming to create the impression that the glove barely fit. In the end, Simpson managed to get the glove on. The problem for the prosecution was that while in theory any observer could rationalize that the rubber liner was probably causing the glove to fit poorly, it *appeared* to be very, very tight—too tight, in fact, to match most people's gut-level, commonsense idea of what a glove should look like when it fits.

Should a poorly staged, easily manipulated glove demonstration be evaluated on the same level as a highly scientific DNA analysis? Of course not. But in the context of Simpson's case, given the mix of subjective ingredients, it "proved" determinative. The prosecution had claimed beyond the shadow of a doubt that the glove belonged to the killer, and that the killer was Simpson. The visual power of the not-so-perfectly-fitting glove created its own "moment of truth" when Simpson's lawyer Johnnie Cochran seized on the moment, crowing, "If it doesn't fit, you must acquit." The "fact" of the glove's insufficiently credible fit became an insuperable obstacle for the prosecution to overcome.

My visual aids enabled me to make the point with immediacy and directness that wealth inequality was not just in the news, not just something that looks terrible on charts; it was here and now, affecting their lives, threatening their children's futures. By making my points for me, my visual aids reduced the rhetorical workload that would otherwise have fallen to my voice, my gestures, and the logic of my argument. My visuals made the case better than I could have done.

As I'd absorbed and ultimately embraced the "artificial" (to use Susan Cain's word) techniques of public speaking, I'd come to see my prior, reflexive devotion to "authenticity" as profoundly misplaced and even destructive. It had felt, at every step, like an act of self-betrayal to question my natural instinct "to be myself" and "to be authentic" with every breath. After all (apart from, perhaps, the worlds of drag and the World Wrestling League), it's hard to imagine a more cherished value in American life. We seek authenticity in our politicians, celebrities, Thai food, craft beer, and travel experiences. We seek it in each other and in ourselves. Our lives are filled with the mass-produced and the ersatz; it's easy to see why we assign meaning and value to products and experiences that feel "real."

But what does it mean, in a world of nearly eight billion inhabitants, to be "authentic"? Does it mean that we manage, against all odds, to be unique and distinct from every other person on Earth? Does it mean we're relentlessly honest, that when people ask us how we are, instead of answering, "Yeah, no, I'm good," as conventional people tend to do, we burst forth with our personal equivalent of *Remembrance of Things Past* by way of an answer? Does our preoccupation with authenticity seem—ever—to make us more so?

I mentioned these thoughts to a friend, and she recommended a book called *The Fall of Public Man,* by sociologist Richard Sennett. I was surprised by how acutely the book, written in the 1970s, describes our present moment of social brittleness—specifically in view of our obsession with authenticity.

In Sennett's depiction, much of ancient social life—among the educated citizenry, at least—took place outdoors, in the public square. The early forums of democracy—trials, elections, and public debates—were rowdy, combative, competitive opportunities for showing off, for demonstrating wit and verbal prowess. The accepted view, not surprising given participants' many years of speech training, was that public life requires a degree of acting.

The modern thinkers and philosophers I'd learned about during my education had championed the importance of fighting back against artifice, falsehood, and convention, of being true to oneself. From Rousseau (natural man versus enfeebling, false society) and Kierkegaard (who wrote of the "massification" and "leveling" pressures imposed on the individual by institutions like the church, the bourgeois state, etc.) on to pretty much every indie rock band I'd ever loved, the message seemed to be that acting is bad and hypocritical. I'd never questioned it.

Sennett's point, which I found intriguing, is that our current, modern obsession with being true and authentic has lured us into a kind of narcissism and an inability to translate and expose our inner selves to the outer world, creating an "imbalance," in Sennett's words, "between public and private life," which has caused us to be vastly less free and, ironically, authentic than we imagine ourselves to be.

Citing population growth and the rise of maturing, capitalist economies as two driving factors (among others), Sennett traces trends in architecture, urban planning, and the theater to show the evolving regard for public space, from venerated locus of democratic well-being to its contemporary association—along with public life in general—as a noisy, degraded, enervating assault upon our personhood. Where once upon a time we felt most alive expressing our fullest capacity out loud, in public, among our peers, modern norms hold the utterly opposite view.

In our retreat from the public square to the social simplicity of our homes and the abdication of interest in maintaining any sense of a "public self," writes Sennett, "we have come to prioritize our inner life and subjectivity as the most sacred, meaningful, and important thing in life." This retreat, however, has left us socially and creatively bereft. As Sennett explains, "The more a person concentrates on feeling genuinely, rather than on the objective content of what is felt," the less skilled we become at seeing objective reality in, of, and for itself. Sennett cites the typical example of the modern politician donning blue jeans to dine or grab a Coors with "the average American family." She *seems* nice and unpretentious. We like her. But what about her tax policy? Captivated as we are with judging how she makes us feel, we lose our ability to assess her real-life impact.

"The more subjectivity becomes an end in itself," Sennett writes, the graver our quibbles become over what does or does not constitute "authentic behavior." If we are conscious of acting, then clearly we're behaving falsely. But if we're trying too hard to be authentic, isn't that another kind of acting? The more obsessed we become with how it *feels* to communicate, the fewer choices we allow ourselves to communicate in terms that succeed objectively.

Sennett's observations about evolving habits of theatergoing are particularly informative to formerly artifice-averse communicators like myself. Through the 1600s, for example, theater was pretty much considered something of an interactive medium. Audience members shouted at actors, haranguing them to repeat the parts they liked and even to respond to demands that they play their parts differently. By the 1800s, however, the separation between actor and public had become codified. Actors acted; the audience's job was to shut up and spectate. After all, actors were trained performers. But what, now, were regular citizens trained to do?

Actors, like rhetoric students, are taught to understand that speech and the performance of character can only be expressed through techniques, patterns, and conventions. Far from trite or banal, Sennett argues, "Convention is itself the single most expressive tool of public life." Focused as we are on subjectivity and authenticity, self-denied the fundamental creative tools of the actor, writes Sennett, we "become inartistic in daily life." In the end, he concludes, we are stranded in our very selves: "We are artists deprived of an art."

As I'd become more versatile at applying my speech lessons to the rigors of daily conversation, I'd curtailed my occasional tendency to overshare. I'd largely reined in my reflexive desire to be "original" and "interesting." It's possible that I talked a bit less than I did before; I certainly talked less for the sake of talking. I'd gained an appreciation for the fact that disagreeing with people goes a lot better if you acknowledge the possibility that they might be right. These alterations to my normal way of talking, you might say, were self-conscious, even artificial; each of them had improved the quality of my social interactions.

Late one evening, as I snuggled with Santi, Isabel emerged from the bedroom into the living room, deeply engaged in what looked like an annoying phone call. In a heartbeat, I knew she was talking to her mother. She covered the phone and whispered, "She's pissed we're not coming for Christmas."

"Mom," she said, returning to her call. "Mom. Mom? I'm really sorry. That's the decision we made."

Her mother had apparently launched into a tirade. Isabel held the phone an inch or two from her ear, and I gestured to her to put it on hold.

Remembering the rhetorical trick I'd learned from the Greeks about verb tense, I said, "Switch the conversation to future tense. Don't let her keep talking about who made what promise." Isabel gave me a dubious look. I continued, "Talk about a solution. What about Presidents' Day weekend? What about Easter?" I made a frowny face and slumped my body, then a happy face, with a gesture of happy uplift, and said, "Past, future!"

When her mom at last tired of talking, Isabel continued in a calmer voice, "Look, Mom, what are you doing for Presidents' weekend? I'd like us all to have something to look forward to."

If rhetoric was a televised sport, like boxing or football, with zooms, freeze-frames, instant replays, and expert commentary, the conversation would have been galvanizing. Every time Isabel shifted verb tense, she said, her mom seemed stunned, like a boxer clocked by a roundhouse punch. She'd sputter, stumble, revive, then lunge anew. Isabel fought back against every sortie. "Mom," she said, "I'm sort of not talking about Christmas anymore, I'm talking about what comes after that." After three rounds of Isabel's pivoting from Christmas to Presidents' Day weekend, her mother ran out of steam. The conversation concluded with Isabel saying, "Great, we'll plan on that."

For a long beat, she looked at me with grudging respect. "If you ever use that trick on me, I'll destroy you."

9

FIND THE PIZZA

When I moved to New York City in 1990, at the age of twenty-six, a friend from Minneapolis and I took an apartment across the street from the Port Authority bus station. At the time it was arguably the most dangerous neighborhood in Manhattan south of Harlem.

The bus station was like a Bosch painting, a multi-dimensional honeycomb of misery, with hundreds of dimly lit tunnels, passageways, and bus docks, collectively (if inadvertently) housing an estimated 1,200 homeless people, many of whom were mentally ill or addicted to drugs.

I approached my new community with the mindset of an anthropologist, fanning out to establish relations with my new neighbors while assessing the cultural and social norms of a new subject population. I was soon playing pool with a former Black Panther named Killer (whose nickname had not been idly chosen) and sharing beers with a prostitute named Joyce, who seemed to end up in a lot of knife fights that weren't her fault. I befriended a poet named DC who claimed to have graduated from Skidmore and to have published a book of poetry housed in the Library of Congress. (I checked. He had.) My closest new friend was a gap-toothed bear of a man named Bumper, a full-time drunk and part-time crack cocaine addict whose proudest credential was a cousin, Maceo Parker, who'd played saxophone for James Brown.

More than once, Bumper laughed at my liberal pieties. He told me about documentary crews from northern European TV stations who'd come to film suffering African Americans in order to depict the cruelty of America (and the superiority of democratic socialism) for their home audience. "They get outta the bus," Bumper laughed, "and we all like, 'Ohhhhh, ohhhh, ohhh, I'm dyin', ain't nobody give me nothing to eat!!'" The film crews invariably rewarded Bumper and his friends with cash as long as they played victim in a media-friendly way—and refrained from mugging the filmmakers.

Bumper had shocked me by forbidding me to give money to beggars, maintaining that they were all alcoholics and drug addicts. I protested. Weren't they deserving of charity? Absolutely not, he insisted. Churches, charities, and city shelters offered plenty of clothes, shelter, and food for anyone willing to play by the rules.

On our tours through the neighborhood, Bumper showed an almost curatorial zeal in demonstrating the different types of beggars for me. One day, we watched a tall, scruffy, roguishly charismatic black man accosting a white husband-and-wife commuter couple. "Look at that handsome devil," said the beggar, pointing to the man for all to see. "What are you, a model?" To the woman, he continued, "That right there?

That's a handsome man." To the man again, he said, "Handsome, give a brother a dollar for a shave and a haircut so I can get myself good-lookin' like you!"

Another time, we passed a bulky, brooding guy with a scar on his neck and a menacing tone alloyed with a note of dubious forbearance. "I ain't robbin' nobody and I ain't stealing," he said, looking way too directly into my eyes. "I'm just trying to get myself something to eat. Gimme a dolla or fifty cents so I can stay outta trouble!"

One day, while riding the subway, we saw a goateed Hispanic man in tattered clothes hobbling through the train leaning on a crutch, bleating piteously, "Oh, Jesus! Pleeease help me! I have AIDS." One of his legs was wrapped with a dirty, blood-stained bandage to which he gestured repeatedly while continuing, "I have not eaten for three and a half days. People, I am so embarrassed to be in this position! This is so humiliating! Please! In the name of Jesus, help me!"

With Bumper's expert guidance I saw how each beggar had—accidentally or on purpose—constructed his own unique pitch, blending threat, humor, charm, anger, vulnerability, grating self-pity, and varying degrees of racial and religious appeal.

The most impressive mendicant in the neighborhood was a short, slight black man with tidy, closely cropped hair whose regular place of business was Fortieth Street and Eighth Avenue. He'd park himself on the ground with his back against the bus station wall, waiting in silence, eyes wide, looking into the distance, proffering an old-fashioned tin beggar's cup. His body was draped with a sorry brown garment; his feet were covered with rags. If you tried your best to tune him out after spotting him, which of course is what most people do when passing beggars, you'd almost certainly find it impossible to shake the impression of otherworldly, vaguely medieval bereftness surpassing ordinary poverty.

I'd seen him quite a few times. He always pulled at my heartstrings. But one afternoon, I passed him with Bumper, who nudged me and started laughing. "Look at his face. Look look look! He putting fucking makeup on!" Indeed, what looked at first glance like a pitiably dirty face turned out to be artfully decorated with theatrical charcoal. Bumper roared. "Look at that fuckin' smock or whatever the fuck that is." Indeed—and here was the key to his otherworldly quality—in a country overflowing with free, barely used clothes of every imaginable style, the beggar had taken the trouble to stitch together a poncho of sorts, cobbled together from burlap potato sacks. Ironically, while his act was by far the most contrived of all the beggars I'd seen, his appeal seemed the least "spun," the least manipulative. It seemed tailored instead to tap directly into a passerby's sense of true charity.

The moment I saw the artistry of his performance and recognized how his and the other beggars' strategies consisted of a set of choices that could in no way have been random, my liberal pieties about the homeless shifted toward something more morally complex. Given the intractable-seeming problem of homelessness, my sympathy remained intact, but I also stopped seeing its victims as hapless. Like citizens of every strata, they wanted something and had developed specifically theatrical strategies for getting it.

My discovery was not merely that people are, or can be, manipulative, but rather that there seemed to be techniques and styles for doing so. For years, I daydreamed about pitching a magazine editor to let me write a piece comparing the beggars' modi operandi with the techniques for sales and negotiation taught by Harvard Business School. My hunch was that regardless of context—rich, poor, formal, or informal—persuasion boils down to a finite number of essentially emotional gambits combining charm, humor, intimidation, flattery, pity, and so on. Such a playbook, once defined, could be fruitfully applied to the threats, promises, entreaties, and appeals of preachers, politicians, terrorists, civil rights leaders, parents, lovers, and kids as a kind of analytical tool. Little did I know, stumbling upon such thoughts at age twenty-six, that I'd opened the door to Rhetoric 101.

Now, twenty-two years later, with five months of Toast-masters under my belt and a rapidly growing appreciation of the usefulness of just such a playbook, I wondered how my life might have unfolded had I, from a young age, been trained in speech and rhetoric, like students of antiquity.

My lack of communication skills had led to myriad mishaps, in public and in private, and a speech-anxious approach to life that shaped my social relations and my overall development as an adult. I've already shown how I interacted with my family. How had my poor speaking skills affected my professional life? As a lifelong freelancer, I'd never opted to be part of a structured professional community. Had I unconsciously avoided "real" jobs out of a reluctance to place myself in a social environment where I would have to make myself understood by others' standards?

I've mentioned the finding that 65 percent of millennials don't feel confident in face-to-face social interactions, and that eight in ten feel more comfortable having a conversation via text or online. Psychologist Tanya Byron feels that the problem lies less in subjects' dependence upon screens than in their inability to get outside their heads. "This high level of overthinking," said Byron, "leads to a lack of robustness and resilience. Anxiety through self-preoccupation is getting in the way of empathy."

I'm not a millennial, but her words describe difficulties from which I suffered long before the mass adoption of electronic communication devices.

Throughout my twenties and thirties, I struggled to handle romantic breakups competently. It seemed beyond my reach to straightforwardly say the words "Hey, I'm sorry, I want to break up." I'd do anything to avoid the conversation. I misbehaved to make my girlfriends break up with me. I let relationships continue long past their expiration date. When it came time to act, I could neither breeze, nor fake, nor put one foot in front of the other and power my way through the conversation. The best I could do was crab-walk, bank-shot, and zig-zag my way through a series of inarticulate half-sentences.

I remember the breakup with a woman I'll call Barbara. After avoiding her calls for a week, I finally called her back. "Sorry I haven't been more available," I said. "I was just thinking."

"Thinking about what?" she asked, warily.

"Well," I said, sighing heavily, in a passive-aggressive attempt to elicit pity. "I'm not really feeling like this is a great time to do this."

" 'This' meaning 'be together'? Have a relationship?"

"Mm. Yeah."

"So, you're breaking up with me?"

"I guess so."

"Okay. Why wouldn't you just say that?"

Armed with what I'd recently learned about public speaking (and a few years' maturity), how could I have approached such moments with greater skill? Starting at square one, I could have thought about my audience. *My audience is someone I care about. Someone whose time I should not waste with vagueness or indirectness.* What might be the purpose for such a phone call? *By the end of our talk, I want Barbara to know that I respect her but that we are no longer going to be seeing each other.*

As my clubmate Hanna Turnquist had said, phone calls follow many of the same rules as formal speeches. Perhaps it might have helped for me to memorize an approximate introduction and conclusion, to think about words I might want to use or avoid, to think about how long the call should be. To my pre-rhetoric manboy self, considering such issues in advance would have felt calculating. But wouldn't the result for both Barbara and me have proved more beneficial?

Between holiday schedules, canceled meetings, and travel for work, I'd missed several meetings. By early December, I'd sat back down to work. My ninth exercise, "Persuade with Power," called for crafting a speech designed to move my audience to action. Success in doing so, the manual explained, would depend on speaking carefully to my audience's concerns, blending fact and emotion to credibly explain the value of my proposed solution.

At first blush, the assignment appeared to be little more than a rehash of earlier exercises. As I began to consider potential topics, however, I realized what distinguished it from previous assignments. My last exercise had forced me to locate *my feelings* about wealth inequality. Now I'd have to locate *my clubmates' feelings,* then speak in a way that meaningfully addressed them. No faking. No glibness.

From a slightly different angle, each and every exercise

had taught precisely the same lesson: The audience is the beginning and end of public speaking. Nine speeches in, you'd
think that I'd be better at directing my thoughts accordingly.
But even now, as I forthrightly set out to locate my audience's
deepest concerns, the first three topics that came to mind had
only to do with myself.

My small family would soon be leaving Minnesota to return to New York, meaning, of course, that I'd soon be leaving Speakeasy. Should I make my speech about that? I'd
groaned about every step of my journey, but my clubmates
had given me an invaluable education. I felt immensely grateful. Did my feelings about leaving have anything to do with
their deepest emotional concerns? No.

Around the same time, I'd been invited by a university in
Alabama to give a talk about one of my books. I felt nervous
and excited by the prospect. I could talk about my anxiety. It
certainly felt important to me. But did it have anything to do
with my clubmates' deepest emotional concerns? No.

A third potential topic came to mind one night during
this time when I received a group email sent by Anne Schiffer:

HAS ANYONE EVER SKYPED FOR A TOASTMAS-
TERS MEETING? IF NOT CAN WE TRY IT? MAYBE
SCOTTY WOULD BE ABLE TO HELP US?

Schiffer was moving to rural Illinois for a few months and
didn't want to lose her connection to the club. The Scotty
she referred to was Scotty Lindholm, the guy I'd beaten in the
Humorous Speech Contest. Lindholm responded:

I tried it as an experiment a couple years ago—I was on
the road. I gave a speech from my hotel room. I could hear

my evaluation just fine, and I could hear everything said by whoever was at the lectern. But without real F2F, I could not really participate in the entire meeting very well.

The next day, Gary Milter chimed in:

Anne,
I don't know that we have. However, I don't think it is a good format for our meeting—better for 1:1 situations.
My thoughts—

Gary

My mind lit up at the prospect of a potential topic. Could Toastmasters work through electronic media? Perhaps my clubmates had strong feelings on the subject. My time with the organization had served as a crash course about eyeballs, pauses, quavers, tone, stance, emphasis, the paying (and not paying) of attention, the face-to-face, real-time quantities and measures of presence that comprised the "art of connecting." The responses to Schiffer's email spoke to the importance of the physical, here-and-now nature of the club; that was what had united us. Interesting, right? Nope. No one at Speakeasy had ever expressed the slightest curiosity about this facet of our activities.

A Toastmaster I'd met earlier in Thousand Oaks, California, had written to announce that she'd be passing through town. Her name was Shana Iravani. She worked as a global account manager for a big tech company. We met for coffee, and I mentioned my difficulty in zeroing in on a good topic. Iravani, a fit woman in her forties with bright green eyes, offered me a seminar in a topic no one had mentioned yet: listening. "Everyone joins Toastmasters with the intention of learning to speak," she said. "The speeches are just the surface. If you want to learn to speak well, focus on listening. Otherwise, it's a waste of time."

Iravani was raised in pre-revolution Iran by an authoritarian father who beat her, trying to instill the lesson that good girls use their brains—not their mouths. "He was brutal," she said. "But I inherited that from him, that toughness. I was very competitive, very quiet—and very insecure." Iravani moved to California in 1980 and became a relentless overachiever, earning two master's degrees before landing a prestigious job at Raytheon, a giant defense contractor. For years, she received steady promotions—until 2004, when her career inexplicably stalled, and six long years passed without advancement. "I couldn't understand what was happening," she told me, with a bemused look. "I'd fought so hard always to be the smartest woman in the room. Now people with half my knowledge were getting promoted above me. It drove me crazy."

After a round of consultations with supervisors and therapists, Iravani confronted the truth. "No one wanted to be around me," she said, laughing. "No one wanted my advice. No one wanted to confide in me. I'd had this idea that if only I had enough knowledge, no one could touch me. But if your job is to manage people, and they don't want to talk to you, it's time to reevaluate your idea of intelligence."

Iravani joined Toastmasters in 2007, hoping to improve her communication skills. True to form, she worked relentlessly, giving as many speeches as her group would allow. In a few short months, she learned how to give a decent speech—then lost her job at Raytheon and, in short order, got sacked from two other jobs. "I still couldn't understand what was happening. I'd worked so hard. I was the smartest person there! I'd done everything except learn how to listen.

"You see this all the time," she continued. "One spouse files for divorce and the other spouse is completely stunned. The problem was brewing for years, but they never listened. You see it in professional situations, and even political, global situations. People can't slow down. They can't see the problem. Which in my case, of course, was me."

One day, after a particularly strained meeting with a volunteer organization Iravani had joined, a colleague took her aside and said, "Shana, you don't respond to what people actually say. You cut them off. Every exchange with you leaves people feeling insulted and misunderstood." Her colleague insisted that Iravani try waiting three seconds before responding to every statement she heard. If she got caught interrupting, she'd have to pay a five-dollar fine.

Iravani gave me a shocked expression: "It was the hardest thing I'd ever learned to do. Much harder than learning to speak in public."

But learning it changed Iravani's life. "In the past," she said, "if someone had a different opinion than mine, I had to answer back. I felt so impatient. I couldn't just let them have their opinion. What I finally realized is that if I can just shut up, absorb what people are saying, and restrain that urge to agree or disagree and respond, I end up wielding far more influence. Because you have to be able to figure out what people need and what they want. If you're busy thinking and trying to be right, you can't do it."

I realized after talking with Iravani that I'd never heard, read, or studied anything about listening. (Remarkably, given the vast quantity of literature about speaking, there's very little about listening.) A quick search online yielded a management bromide called the 80/20 rule (the idea being that a good manager spends 80 percent of his or her time listening and 20 percent talking). But the best thing I found came from an article about a suicide hotline in San Francisco invented by a man named Bernard Mayes (who, coincidentally, was one of the founders of NPR).

In the 1970s, Mayes discovered that in their final, downward drift toward death, future suicide victims frequently find themselves abandoned. At the moment they most need connection and someone to talk to, their families, friends, and even mental health professionals can't bear the weight of hearing about their problems one more time. *It's just too hard to listen.*

Mayes surmised that if a special cadre of people could be trained to listen to their woes in a radically detached way—with a technique he eventually called "exquisite listening"—perhaps some of them might be dissuaded from suicide. The group he founded, the San Francisco Suicide Prevention Center, receives 70,000 calls a year.

According to Eve Meyer, the center's executive director, hotline callers suffer from a wide array of issues, from financial stress to chronic physical pain, drug dependency, and varying forms of mental illness causing depression, delusions, and hallucinations. Callers from foreign cultures are motivated by concerns that native-born Americans might find bewildering: A sister was raped, and they believe she has brought shame to the family; an uncle was charged with embezzlement, and the family name has been ruined. The stigma is unbearable, and suicide seems the logical answer.

The hotline is staffed by ten full-timers and a hundred volunteers, none of whom boast medical degrees, and all of whom are trained, like crack rhetoricians, to set their egos and preconceptions aside and *listen*. As Meyer explained, "Our clients already have the answers. They know their options far better than we do. Our job is to help them locate it."

For example, said Meyer, "If a caller is hallucinating and is seeing something the rest of us do not see, such as monsters in the refrigerator, you would not, for example, argue with them about whether monsters exist, or get into a discussion about their state of mind. Your only purpose is to help them find their best option. So a good question might be 'Well, where are you standing? Where's the monster? Can you get to the front door to get away from it? What did you do the last time the monster came out of the refrigerator? Are you taking any medication? Is the monster somewhere in between you and your medication?'"

The root of exquisite listening, Meyer explained, lies in suspending ordinary preconceptions and responses, stilling our natural impulse to judge, argue, and engage and directing our intellectual energies toward one goal: securing the physical survival of the caller.

"Let's say someone calls," said Meyer, "someone with a mood disorder, depression, whatever, and they insist that there is simply no point in living, no point in going on." How do you convince them otherwise? "You try," Meyer explained, "to find out the thing that's stronger than they are, the dream, the belief—whatever pulls them along when their spiritual muscles are giving out. It may be pizza. It may be the person's grandmother. You're hunting," she said, "for what I call the diamonds—the buffers, the people or things they love, that make life worthwhile. And it's an art, hunting for it. Because you can't just ask, 'What gives you pleasure in life?' They've lost sight of it. So you have to do a lot of listening until you find the thing. You say, 'Tell me about your family. How has your family treated you through this?' 'Well, they've all been awful.' 'All of them?' 'All but my grandmother.' You have to find the grandmother. You have to find the pizza. I've actually talked people into a pizza instead of death.''

The story piqued my interest in part because I'd been pondering the subject of listening, but also, again, for the same reason my cousin Bill's story had drawn my attention to the subject of public speaking. I found it fascinating that words—language skills—could solve problems usually relegated to the domain of psychiatry. Only after digesting Iravani's advice and the example of exquisite listening did I absorb what they meant for me: I'd been sitting in different rooms, alone, driving myself crazy, thinking about my clubmates' deepest needs. It hadn't occurred to me to stop thinking and to try listening to them.

I called my group's old-timers, Al Hoffman, Gordon Andersen, and Margo Forster, to ask for a chat. An hour before our next meeting, we gathered around the conference table in our temporary meeting room.

I'd asked them in earlier conversations why they'd joined. I'd learned enough about their personalities to know that asking them directly to tell me their deepest feelings wasn't likely to pay off. So I planned to ask them about the club's history, and how it had changed over time. Between them, I'd calculated, they'd accumulated almost one hundred years of membership. I decided to start with that.

Speakeasy, as you might imagine, had hardly been a magnet for high drama. Once, Forster recalled, the club had had to purge a lecherous newcomer for making unwanted advances. Hoffman remembered a Miss Minnesota contestant who repeatedly tried to use the club as a sounding board for her pageant speech—without paying her dues. Andersen smiled at the memory. "Yeah. She bamboozled us. Didn't win the pageant, though."

The most dramatic moment in Speakeasy history, they said, occurred in 2004, when membership dwindled to four— Andersen, Hoffman, Forster, and Forster's husband, Burt. As Hoffman explained, the rules governing club charters were very strict. If Speakeasy's membership had remained below six people for another semester, the main office in California would have revoked the club's charter.

For four months, Hoffman, Andersen, and Forster (Burt's work schedule prevented him from coming most nights) filled the two-hour meeting time by playing multiple roles: Toastmaster, Sergeant at Arms, Educational VP, Evaluator, Timer, Grammarian, Ah Counter, and Master Evaluator, improvising what to talk about. "Most weeks," Forster said, "we'd kinda come in here and just wonder, 'Hmm. How many are we gonna be tonight?'"

"It wasn't really always a *formal* meeting," Hoffman recalled with a sheepish look. "I'd eat a sandwich. We'd drink some pop. We'd talk. Well, Gordon mostly talked. And then we'd go home." Andersen and Forster twinkled at the memory. Andersen smirked. "I've always been something of a ham."

On the odd weeks that a newcomer showed up, the group assigned him or her a role or two and snapped into full Toastmasters protocol, rising before speaking, addressing one another as "fellow Toastmasters" and the guest as "distinguished guest," inviting the newcomer to join in.

When I asked what motivated them to show up week after week, Hoffman's brow creased. "We had to show up. If no one was here and a visitor came by, how would they know to come back?" He looked almost pained. "If we just put up a sign saying 'Meeting Canceled,' we'd never have gotten the new members we needed to keep going!" I'd never seen him express such strong emotion.

As luck would have it, they explained, the economy soon took a dive. As often happens when times get tough, a surge of prospective members began to arrive, desperate to hone their job interview skills. Membership's been healthy ever since.

Members began filtering in for our meeting. We'd run out of time. I hadn't quite figured out their deepest needs, as I'd hoped. But maybe they'd already said enough.

Later, on the drive home, I thought about what they'd said. If I took their story at face value, what I got from the old-timers was a sense that engagement was highly important to them. The younger people I'd met had offered a host of reasons for joining: they'd wanted to learn to give speeches and to overcome shyness. But they'd also joined to overcome compulsive funniness, to stop yelling at subordinates, to learn to handle criticism in meetings, to improve their ability to socialize at parties, to prepare and deliver marriage proposals, to learn how to "be authentic in poignant moments." Wasn't this all another way of saying "to engage"?

I started thinking about the purpose of my speech. What did I want to persuade them to do? It seemed simple enough: If it was deeply important for them to engage, why not ask them to . . . engage more?

My "ask" would be to get them to talk to people they don't know.

With my later speeches, I'd found it less and less necessary to write out every word as I had in the past. If I landed correctly upon an appropriate topic, purpose, and organizational plan, then memorized my introduction and conclusion, I could generally sketch my ideas on a couple of sheets of lined paper.

I decided to introduce my speech by discussing some of the scary statistics I'd found about isolation and declining civic life in America. With a homemade graph depicting the decreasing number of friends claimed by the average American over the last fifty years, I made my point: Isolation is bad. Simplistic, perhaps, but it set me up nicely to state my ask: What might happen if we start engaging with people we don't know?

I told a story about a call I'd made recently to a 1-800 number to fix a problem I'd been having with my phone. I was angry, annoyed, and eager to bash the telephone operator to express my rage about the phone company's bad service. I decided instead, just for an exercise, to try being friendly. I asked the operator how he was doing. I asked if he was in the Philippines. I said hi in Tagalog. It was nothing big, but I knew I'd probably made his day better than if I'd been a jerk. The payoff for me, however, was that engaging had made me happier than if I'd gone through the call like a grouch or a robot.

I continued with a list of opportunities my clubmates might consider for engaging with strangers: They could try making eye contact; they could try making a phone call instead of sending an email; they could try making conversation with someone at the gas station or at the hospital. They could even try engaging better with family members. As I led up to my conclusion, I said, "You might think that I'm asking you to be false, to indulge in a kind of meaningless friendliness." But think, I concluded, "of all the times and places where you *don't* engage, where you walk on by, where you tune people out. It takes energy not to care. It takes energy to tune people out. So I'll ask you once again: Try to engage with the people you pass by in daily life. What's the harm?"

My speech was by far the easiest and most comfortable yet. I stumbled once or twice. But when I stumbled now, it didn't bother me much. I'd realized, over the course of several speeches, that audiences don't really care if you're perfectly smooth. They care far more that you're speaking to them, meeting them on their level, and speaking in a way that respects their interest. A couple of hiccups here and there don't derail that.

"Well, John," beamed Gordon Andersen, stepping to the lectern to deliver my evaluation. "You really leaned into it, and it shows." Andersen, never one to pull punches, praised my choice of topic and my forceful, confident delivery. I'd used clear examples with vivid word choices, I'd gotten my hands out of my pockets, and overall my body language had "straightened out." "Now," he continued, "much as I'd like to, I can't give you a full pass yet. And that's because it took you just a bit too long to let us know what the heck you wanted us to do. I didn't know what it was until somewhere in the middle." As always, Andersen was right. But I left the meeting in a good mood, happy to have connected and done my competent best.

Three nights later, on Christmas Eve, my real-life public speaking skills would be put to the ultimate test. My family—brother, sister, mother—had gathered to celebrate the holidays, along with old friends of my mother's I'll call Joe and Elizabeth, who'd flown in from Las Vegas.

As we hustled about, setting tablecloths, polishing gravy bowls, and sous-chef-ing for my mom, strands and sparks of disconnected conversation flew in every direction.

My mother was charming, amply able to enjoy herself while producing a sixteen-pound turkey, brussels sprouts, stuffing, gravy, scalloped potatoes, asparagus, and salad and tossing off a steady stream of holiday-themed non sequiturs. My brother managed to turn even conversations about Christmas carols to his recent songwriting trip to Nashville. Isabel nimbly stayed out of the fray, attending to Santi, while my sister googled gravy recipes, offering my mother tips for improving the gravy she's made for forty years.

The ultimate curveball of the evening, however, was thrown by Elizabeth, the sole evangelical Christian among us. "John," she said, "how about saying a few words for grace? So many blessings!"

I hadn't, for a moment, prepared myself for such a request. I'd heard grace said at many a meal, at Isabel's parents' home and many others. Nor was I afraid of religious sentiment. For years I'd had a steady morning meditation ritual which began with random readings from religions around the world. I'd been obsessing, learning, practicing, and preparing to speak in public for months. But I hadn't prepared for *this*. I gulped. And then, faster than my mind could fill with clutter, I cleared it.

"Thank you all for being here," I began. "We're very lucky to have this food, which my mother so graciously prepared. This chance to have everyone in the family in the same room at the same time is kind of a miracle. Let's give it up for airplanes. But let's also give it up for the fact that all of us are in good health, including Santi. I'm so glad you guys"—I gave a nod to the whole table—"could make it. Am I missing something?" The smiles and head shakes indicated no.

No one seemed put out or alarmed. Everyone started eating. I'd said what I had to say. There was nothing left to think about but the food. Amen!

10

TOWARD JUSTICE AND HARMONY

We'd rolled into the New Year, and I was approaching the end of my time with Toastmasters. My tenth and final exercise would prove, perhaps, hairiest of all. The goal: to write and deliver an inspirational speech. An inspirational speech, my manual explained, often uses words like "you" and "we" to unite an audience and to motivate them to improve personally, emotionally, professionally, or spiritually. Examples might include a political speech, a speech for a business conference, and high school and college commencement addresses.

In addition to zeroing in once again on my clubmates' needs, desires, and aspirations, I'd now have to match them up with my own, then demonstrate a higher degree of passion, enthusiasm, sincerity, and urgency than in any of my previous speeches.

If choosing a topic for the previous two exercises had proven tricky, the current task seemed insuperable. From earliest childhood, I'd hated to be told what to do, much less what to believe. I'd tried my best, by no means perfectly, to steer clear of telling others what to believe or how to behave.

Now, charged with doing just that, what in the world could I, with a straight face, possibly urge anyone to do? Certainly, I could think of actions *I* might find inspiring: *Let's all quit our jobs, move off the grid, live off the land, and stop contributing to global warming! Let's all have more and better sex! Let's all be more polite! Let's all be nicer to kittens!* All kidding aside, however, it seemed incredibly daunting. What inspiring action could I earnestly recommend to my clubmates that would transcend the motivational and inspirational dreck and go beyond saying, "Yeaaaahhh!! Be all you can be! You're awesome!"

A search online for "inspirational speeches" yielded dozens of popular examples. I found J. K. Rowling's highly regarded 2008 Harvard commencement address, titled "The Fringe Benefits of Failure, and the Importance of Imagination." The speech begins with Rowling's humble beginnings, touches upon the inevitability of failure (yes, even for Harvard graduates), then discusses Rowling's pre–Harry Potter work with African torture victims during a stint at Amnesty International. Citing the experience as a pivotal moment in her development, Rowling suggests that empathizing with those less fortunate extends our perspective beyond the conventional, materially defined, hamster-wheel context of success versus failure. Calling upon her audience's intellectual, economic, and moral power, she urges them to harness their imaginations in order to find their sense of mission. "We do not need magic to change the world, we carry all the power we need inside ourselves already: We have the power to imagine better."

I also found Steve Jobs's celebrated 2005 Stanford commencement address, called "How to Live Before You Die," in which he urges his audience, "Live each day like it's your last." Using the gripping story of his tremendous professional reversals of fortune and his then-recent diagnosis of cancer, Jobs makes a moving case: The surest way to have a meaningful life is to stick to our guns, live by our own values, avoid dogma (our own as well as others'), and follow our hearts and intuition.

Finally, I watched Oprah Winfrey's classic 2008 address at Stanford, in which she discusses the value of failure. "Your education isn't ending here," she counsels. "In many ways, it's only just begun." Describing life on Earth as a giant classroom, Winfrey says that the key to getting ahead—and surviving life's inevitable ups and downs—is learning to pay close attention to what feels right. "When you're supposed to do something or not supposed to do something, your emotional guidance system lets you know," Winfrey advises. "Every wrong decision I've ever made was a result of me not listening to the greater voice of myself. If it doesn't feel right, don't do it. That's the lesson."

Synopsized on the page, the speeches seem lighter than when viewed on video. What made them work, aside from the weight of their speakers' tremendous real-life achievements, was the warmth, competence, and earnestness with which they expressed themselves. In theory, there should be no reason why I could not concoct something similar.

As I sat down to work one last time looking out over now-frozen Lake Calhoun and began thinking once again about my clubmates' emotional needs, it struck me that I'd missed something crucial during the previous exercise. It felt right to zero in on my fellow Toastmasters' desire for engagement with the world. But in the end, I reflected, my suggestion—that they should "talk to people they don't know"—felt somewhat abstract. Had any of them tried it as a result of my speech? It seemed unlikely, precisely because I hadn't spelled out a specific-enough reward for doing so.

I circled back to Andersen, hoping he might shed light on whatever I was missing. When I asked him how his Toastmasters skills affect his daily life, he paused for a moment, then answered with more enthusiasm than I'd anticipated: "It keeps you sharp! It keeps you from getting run over by life!" Continuing, he said:

> I was in the post office yesterday. They had only one counter open. And the guy who was working there had a stack of blue envelopes about a foot high that he was working on, and he was taking his time, spending about three or four minutes on each one. The line was getting longer and longer. I was about third in line. And at one point, I said the thing everybody was thinking: "Are you going to do all of those things right now?" And he said, "Yes, sir." And I said, "Don't you have anybody in back who could help you?" Well, he yelled to the back, and finally, a second clerk came up. I realize this isn't exactly leading a revolution, but it occurred to me later: In my own small way, I used my voice to benefit humanity. I know the people in line with me appreciated the fact that I'd spoken up.

Andersen wasn't done yet. "A Toastmaster speaks up! We ask questions! What happens when people stop being able to ask questions? Some people are afraid to ask their doctor to explain their examination results. If you think about going to meetings at the school board or the city council, stepping up to the microphone and expressing your opinion—that's democracy! And it takes a certain kind of courage. Sometimes, you just have to holler, 'Hey, what's going on here?'"

Andersen's description of Toastmasters' helpfulness in daily life fit nicely with my own inspired feelings about speech training: that it could serve as a kind of medicine. Why not enlarge upon Andersen's thoughts and bring them home to the rest of the club? The purpose of the speech, I decided, would be to inspire my audience to use their Toastmasters knowledge in daily life as a kind of medicine, a kind of force for good, for connection, but also as a way to solve problems.

In no time at all, I'd thrown together a speech beginning with the words "Today I'm going to talk to you about the power and the benefits of using Toastmasters' techniques in daily life."

I told the story of my cousin Bill, of his many years in the basement, of his loneliness and isolation, and of how joining the organization had given him the tools to meet his future wife. I discussed an article I'd found describing the vastly increased effectiveness of calling politicians on the phone versus sending them email. According to congressional aides and staffers, the fact of having to respond to a real person makes the office aware of public opinion. Email? Not so much.

I used the story of a near fight with an old friend—deftly avoided, thanks to careful speaking on my part—to describe my own experience with Toastmasters and what membership in Speakeasy had given me. I'd learned how to write speeches, but I'd also learned to get through daily life situations with less stress, more grace, and yes, in the end, a far greater sense of feeling connected in everyday life—with my partner, with my family, with my club, and even with my preverbal kid.

By way of conclusion, I recounted something Debbi

Fields Rose (of Mrs. Fields Cookies) told me when I'd interviewed her. She said, "Oh, John, you're going to be great at explaining public speaking for the younger generation. Because you're not me. I'm the cheerleader type. People call me the Energizer Bunny. But you're like, 'I don't even believe in this stuff. And it *still* works!'"

Her comment was deadly accurate. I'd joined Toastmasters driven by my intellectual curiosity about an art form that had been a *really big deal* since antiquity. I had a sense that it might be a *really big deal* for people to learn it once again. These facts, at the outset, had nothing to do with me, however, personally or emotionally. The subject—of language, communication, rhetoric, connection—was so large that, like most people alive today, I just couldn't see it. The benefits I'd received from it had come as something of a shock.

As I discovered at my first Toastmasters meeting, it's alienating and fraught to join a group of strangers. The reality of "active participation" and learning to "be yourself"—and all the related subtasks like listening, tolerating, accommodating, adjusting, moderating, and modulating one's body and voice that distinguish face-to-face communication from electronic communication—had indeed imbued me with a new sense of self. I *think* I speak better than I did before joining. But I *know* I'm less alienated from humanity. "Strangers" have ceased to be quite so strange; they are my fellow citizens. I am, to borrow from the ancient Greek definition of shyness, no longer so perplexed about how to interact with strangers—and everyone else.

My speech, in the end, felt like a mixed bag, several steps shy of eloquence but blissfully free of calamity or stress. My evaluator, Alex Čapek, whose dark, ironic sense of humor seemed often to match my own, had served as comic relief during my stint with Speakeasy. As he commended my topic, organization, word choice, vocal variety, and body language, I tensed up, waiting for the other shoe to drop. It didn't. "I found your speech genuinely inspiring," he said, as if surprised to hear himself say the words. "You managed to express your serious feelings with humor, and ultimately tell us something meaningful. So thanks. I know you're going back to New York soon, and I speak for the group when I say: You'll be missed."

By mid-January, Isabel, Santi, and I had resumed life in New York. Life was warmer and noisier. It seemed strange and even wrong to not see a lake outside the window. Isabel went back to work, and I sat down at my small, New York–size table to prepare for my first real speech outside Toastmasters, an address I'd been hired to give at Alabama's Auburn University, for a group of some five hundred students. The school had invited me to discuss a book about modern slavery that I'd published in 2008.

In the past, my speech preparation regimen had consisted of feeling bad for three or four days while randomly reworking my speech materials. It wasn't fun, but it felt a lot like diligence. Never mind that the process had never helped me give a decent speech.

This time, I googled the university and looked for recent campus news. I researched their history, learned about the departments I'd be meeting with, and took a look at the kinds of students who came to the school. I even researched their sports teams and football team song. I wrote the events coordinator who'd hired me and asked her about the students I'd be speaking to. What classes were they coming from? What did they already know about my topic? What were their politics like? Bit by bit, I began to get a sense of who I'd be addressing.

Deciding upon the purpose of the speech was easy: I wanted the students to understand that slavery still exists, that it's been the norm throughout history, and that unchecked wealth inequality looks suspiciously likely to lead us toward a world we're lucky to have escaped from. I wanted to inform them that fighting against slavery—now—was something they might want to consider.

When I'd talked about the book in the past, I'd sometimes played a very crude, scratchy audiocassette recording of a Mexican farmworker shrieking in Spanish on the phone to a South Florida 911 operator. The farmworker was traveling with a group of fellow farmworkers that had come under attack from a labor contractor named El Diablo who would later be convicted of slavery. In the recording, the worker can be heard begging for help in Spanish, while the English-speaking 911 operator berates him for not speaking English. This, to me, captured the sound of modern slavery.

As a deeply authentic guy (and maybe a slightly lazy guy as well), I believed it would have been pretentious to improve or "manipulate" the recording. Knowing full well that it was hard to hear, that most of my listeners couldn't understand Spanish, and that the context of the recording was dense and hard to grasp, I'd played the recording with a cheap plastic cassette player held against the microphone. My audiences probably never had a clue what they were hearing.

I now took the trouble to digitize, edit, and clean my recording, adding subtitles and translations to project overhead. I wrote an introduction to ensure that every word of the recording would be crystal clear. I rehearsed my speech, practiced using my visual aids, then timed several run-throughs, alone and with friends on the phone.

The flight to Alabama was pleasant. Untroubled by mind-bending anxiety, I was able to notice the mild southern weather and the well-appointed campus. At speech time, I introduced myself by telling a story about my first trip to Auburn thirty years earlier, hitchhiking. A man in a rusty brown Dodge pickup had invited me to ride with his common-law wife and stepson to their home to go fishing in their man-made bass pond. The details of the story, I said, would have to wait for another time, but the upshot was that the guy decided—just for fun—to fire his shotgun inside the house while aiming perilously close to his common-law wife and her kid. As the guy explained, things had been a little tense. It seemed like a jaunty way to lighten the mood.

The crowd (college kids who, presumably, came from families who didn't blow shotguns off indoors) was shocked, but the shock turned to amusement when I congratulated them, and the town of Auburn generally, for getting their shit together since my first visit. The line got a laugh and then, more sincerely, I thanked them for inviting me and allowing me to talk to them about a subject so important to me.

Having set the mood with a joke, I played my perfectly audible recording. It proved to be a suitably scary introduction to the world I would be describing. The students were rapt. The speech was comfortable, easy, relaxed, and lively.

I'd given dozens of talks years earlier, when my book had come out. At the end of each one, during the Q&A period, audience members invariably exclaimed, "Wow. We never knew that slavery still exists. That's terrible. What can we do?" I never had a good answer, but as a reporter (not an activist) I felt that this wasn't my problem. Instead of offering a helpful answer, I typically rattled off more horror stories about bad labor conditions. My audience probably left my presentations as depressed as I did.

For the Auburn students, I'd found three good, meaningful, appropriate solutions and worked them into my speech. When questions arose about them later in the presentation, I had the answer. Everyone left on a positive note, including me. I flew back home, thrilled to have participated. After a lifetime of feeling vapid, unfulfilled, embarrassed, and regretful after every public speech occasion, I felt . . . *fine*.

One night in February, back at home, Isabel and I went out to dinner with friends. It was a pleasant New York evening with a highly educated, self-possessed group of creative professionals. Someone asked me what I was working on, so I explained. The subject—learning how to connect in a time of such disconnection—inevitably aroused great interest. Just as inevitably, however, when I mentioned the time commitment and emotional struggle required to learn to speak in public, interest fell off. One of our tablemates asked me how, in today's busy world, people found time for anything as whimsical as Toastmasters.

I recalled the intense sense of loyalty and civic engagement Andersen, Forster, and Hoffman had described, the pleasure they'd taken in lending assistance to new Toastmasters, and the fierce struggle I'd seen waged by most of my fellow clubmates, week after week, as they clawed their way through speech anxiety.

I looked around the restaurant. Perhaps a third of the diners were staring at their phones—hunched, disengaged, bored, idle. I answered without thinking: "Umm, 'cuz this electronic stuff is a bummer." I paused. "It's actually going to kill us."

I hadn't really known I'd felt that strongly, but the moment I said the words, I realized they accurately described my feelings. My friends had never, ever seen me express myself with such passion. Startled by my remark, one of them asked, "So, would you actually recommend Toastmasters?" "Yeah!" I said. "I'd recommend it like I'd recommend water."

Toastmasters had changed the way I think about speech, but it had also changed the way I think about people, time, and even the meaning of life. I'd had a bit of a vision: What do people typically grab on to in their final moments before death? Every account I've heard mentions flashbacks of people, places, and real-life moments that meant the most to the person at the moment of dying. Will any of us, during those final seconds, seize upon the great emails and text messages we've shared?

As I'd prepared for my final speech, I'd called my cousin Bill in Iowa to check in on him and see how he and Debbie were doing. I found him full of news. They'd gone on a series of trips—to Germany, to Texas, then to Rome to attend Mass at Saint Peter's. Back in Dyersville, Bill had taken a job at the local church as a custodian and as a greeter before and after services. As he talked, I couldn't help thinking: It all came back to the day he joined Toastmasters.

Curious to glean every possible detail about his first encounter with Debbie that I might have missed before, I asked him to tell me about it once again. At the time of their meeting, he'd been living alone in a four-bedroom house for twelve years. "I must admit," he said, "I liked my own company quite well. But the place was empty, and there was, I must say, a wee bit of loneliness about it."

One sunny afternoon in June, Bill took a drive to nearby Marshall Park. As mentioned earlier, he'd heard the park staged singles meets on Sundays. When he saw Debbie, seated on a bench overlooking the Mississippi River, he paused to gather his nerve to talk to her, reasoning to himself, "Well, we are all in this particular park for the same reason. I'll introduce myself and see how it goes." So he did. "Hello. I'm Bill. I noticed you sitting here. It's such a lovely day. I wondered if you'd mind if I sit here as well."

After that, he told me, "One word led to another. The next thing I knew, I asked her if she wanted to go out to a dance and she said, 'Sure.' And that," he laughed, "was the end of that."

But wait, I said. His speech, first words, his introduction— had he rehearsed them? Had he thought them out in advance, like they teach at Toastmasters?

"Oh, golly," he answered immediately. "Yes. I couldn't have done it any other way."

People hadn't believed me when I told them Bill's story. In an age of increased wariness about talking to strangers, it seemed unthinkable that a guy like Bill had approached a woman he'd never met, started talking to her out of the blue, and obtained a positive result. He'd transformed his life from utter loneliness to one of warmth and joy by learning some basic speech techniques.

I'd stumbled into the subject of rhetoric with no idea what it was or what it meant beyond its common, modern connotation as "fancy talk" or, worse, "bullshit." I hope I've made it clear: Rhetoric is the means by which we find our voices.

By "we," I mean shy people. But I also mean we as a nation of warring, divided factions and motley demographics: Christians, Sikhs, libertarians, Democrats, Republicans, hippies, students, old people, trans people, Flat Earth Society members, and tax collectors—people who may loathe or misunderstand one another but still need to figure out how to pave the roads they share, pick up the garbage, and—why not?—take action to avoid global warming.

I'd searched for years for a way to express the relationship between rhetoric and justice I'd absorbed from Aristotle. His thoughts and theories on the subject were beautiful, but nearly impenetrable and impossible to explain. Several months after graduating from Toastmasters, I found a better description.

A thousand years before the Greeks came along, the Egyptians had assigned rhetoric to Maat, the goddess of order and harmony. Maat's job description included keeping the cosmos in check, holding the stars in their proper orbits, regulating relations among the fractious gods around her, and smoothing troubles among the warring tribes of humankind below. Human beings, in turn, served Maat by arguing—by using rhetoric to fix things.

Word by word, hour by hour, with every complaint, command, joke, and request, we strive to correct the people around us, to cadge our share of love, to cajole, to soothe, to repeat ourselves, to be heard, to get what we need, and to make things right. And in so doing, we do Maat's work, nudging, coaxing, adjusting ourselves and those around us toward permanent justice and harmony.

APPENDIX

Five Steps to Help You Give a Great Speech

Many readers open a book like this looking for simple guidance about surviving their next speech, report, or presentation. Here, for your benefit, is the briefest possible outline of how to do so.

Step 1: Think about your audience.

In the words of Aristotle: The audience is the beginning and the end of public speaking.

Tempting as it is to prepare for a speech by obsessing over your anxieties or your material, the ancient approach to public speaking consisted of doing the opposite. I'll divide the process into three general steps: thinking about your audience; writing for your audience; and using your voice and body to connect to your audience and to enhance their ability to understand you.

The first task in thinking about your audience is to sit down . . . and . . . *think about your audience.* Before finalizing your topic or beginning to draft your speech, ask yourself the following questions, and write down your answers.

- How many people will there be?
- What race, religion, gender, nationality, and ethnicity are they?

- How old are they?
- How educated are they?
- What's the occasion for your speech? Why have they chosen you to speak to them?
- What do they know about you and your topic?
- Look at the room (or a picture of the room) where you'll be speaking, so you have a clear idea of who will sit where and what it will be like to speak to them. Will you, for example, need a microphone?
- What time of day will it be, will they be hungry, what will they have been doing before they hear you?
- Do they have any printed material or web access to information you may be presenting?

If you've made it this far, you've begun to shift your focus from yourself to your audience. The next step will bring you even closer to seeing things from their point of view.

Step 2: Define your purpose for speaking.

You're sitting at your desk, or in your car, or perhaps in your prison cell awaiting a parole hearing. You're ready to start writing. But wait.

Before you do, ask yourself: What is my purpose for speaking? What do I want my audience to know or do as a result of my speech? Formulate your answer as a single sentence: *As a result of my talk, they will know X, and respond by doing Y.*

As a result of my presentation about my company's analytics platform, they will know that we can help them be better at their job, and they will respond by hiring us to consult on their portfolios.

As a result of my slide show about my family's disastrous trip to the North Dakota Badlands, they will be amused, and they will respond by preparing better than I did for their next family vacation.

As a result of my admittedly not-so-interesting quarterly sales report, they will learn the Q3 figures for my territory;

AND they will notice that I'm considerably more dignified than Justin, with his neurotic little laugh, a fact that they will remember through the year-end review.

It may be that your purpose is merely *to inform* or *to entertain* and that you're not asking your audience to do anything in particular. Either way, you need to know exactly why you're talking. If a slide, statistic, joke, or anecdote in your speech doesn't serve your purpose, cut it.

To return to Aristotle, people listen—people anywhere, to any speaker anywhere—for one reason: *to be happy.* If this seems odd, think how it feels to listen to someone prattling away about a subject you don't care about. Does it make you happy? From your audience's perspective, when you speak in a way that isn't directly relevant to their happiness, *you're the prattler.*

Your audience needs to know three things:

1. What you're talking about
2. Why they should care
3. What's in it for them

The point is not that your talk itself must promise immediate, eternal, and infinite bliss for your audience. But every decision you make about your speech must demonstrate that you're talking for their benefit, not yours.

Step 3: Outline and organize your speech.

Speeches and presentations are typically composed of an introduction, three to five main parts, and a conclusion. These parts should not be recited like a list, but must be organized around a larger structure. Some common organizational structures include:

- Chronological: explains your topic along a timeline, with a beginning, a middle, and an end. *Today I'm going to talk about the history of pasta-making, from its origins as a handmade product in ancient China and Italy to its current manufacture in state-of-the-art factories around the world.*
- Spatial: lays out your topic according to physical or directional relationship. *Today I'm going to talk about different types of noodles you can enjoy in Texas, Luxembourg, and northern Malaysia.*

- Topical: arranges information according to areas within a larger topic or category. *Today I'm going to talk about the grains most commonly used to make pasta: semolina wheat, rice, and barley.*
- Cause and effect: explains the causes of or reasons for a phenomenon and the resulting effects (or vice versa). *Today I'm going to talk about rising obesity rates in Texas, Luxembourg, and northern Malaysia, which scientists have increasingly attributed to the overconsumption of refined grains.*
- Problem-solution: defines a problem and articulates a solution. *Today I'm going to talk about how sufferers of obesity around the world can benefit from eating pasta made from garbanzo beans, which contains fewer carbs and more protein than traditional pastas.*

Whichever structure you choose, tell your audience early in your speech what it is: *Here's what I'm going to talk about, and here's how I'm going to talk about it.* As you proceed through the different parts of your speech, explain at every transition where you are: *I've told you now about how we eat noodles in Texas. Now I'm going to tell you about how those crazy Luxembourgers eat noodles!*

If it seems inefficient to waste precious time talking about *how* you're talking, instead of using every available second to transmit your message itself, consider the age-old adage, "Tell 'em what you're gonna tell 'em; tell 'em; then tell 'em that you told 'em." To return once more to Aristotle, public speaking has less to do with conveying information than it does with demonstrating credibility. By delivering on your promise to talk a certain way, you prove yourself to be a reliable tour guide.

Step 4: Compose your speech.

Use Words Effectively

Experts have historically been divided about whether it's better to write down every single word of a speech (and even to memorize it) or merely to sketch out the main points. There are pros and cons with both methods; either way, on the most basic level, your speech will be composed with words. Here are four guidelines for using them well:

1. People are bad at listening—especially in a crowd. Do everything you can to help them hear and understand you. Use

short words, sentences, and paragraphs to express your ideas. Use physical, concrete, vivid images that appeal to the senses, and active verb choices in place of abstract or passive language.

2. As you write, and later as you practice, eliminate every word that fails to impart your exact and intended meaning. This means filler words like *um, ah, like, y'know,* and so on. But it also includes:

- Sneaky, nonperforming words (like "just" and "really")
- Lazy catch-phrases and clichés ("at the end of the day," "at this point in time," "It is what it is," and so forth)
- Business jargon ("disrupt," "learnings," and every other nauseating bit of it, all of which is a fig leaf for genuine thinking and self-expression)
- Pretentious, puffed-up word choices ("utilize" instead of "use," for instance)
- Bloated or inexact expressions ("five or six" or "about six" or "half a dozen" in lieu of "six")
- Slang terms, foreign words, or subcultural expressions your audience doesn't understand.

3. Be specific. Your family and friends know what you mean when you say "big," "rich," "dark," "painful," "successful," and so on. But these everyday terms lose traction when spoken to a varied audience of strangers. A military veteran or trauma survivor, for example, might have a different idea of "painful" than your average clutter consultant. "A big house" means vastly different things to different kinds of people. If by "big house" you mean not, for example, jail, and not, for example, a 3,500-square-foot house but a 1,700-square-foot house, say so. If by "dark" you mean "midnight blue" and not "jet black," take the trouble to make it clear. Words in a speech work best when everyone in the room understands the exact same thing.

4. As you draft the ideas, metaphors, examples, and jokes that will make up your speech, compose them using terms and ideas drafted from the cognitive lexicon of your audience. Are you using inches as a unit of measure when addressing an audience that uses the metric system? Convert to their unit of measure.

On a more conceptual level, if you're speaking to a group of Iowans while fundraising for a pediatric cancer organization, find examples of kids from Iowa who have suffered from the kind of cancer you're trying to cure. If you're speaking to a group in Fujian, China, find examples of kids from Fujian.

While words are the essential building blocks of any presentation, other common speech components include the use of data and visual aids.

Use Data Effectively

As Aristotle observed, logic and facts rarely and barely move crowds the way we think they do. Data and other forms of evidence can be handy for getting a point across, but to use them effectively, the following guidelines should be observed:

- Use data sparingly. A handful of facts and figures is usually enough for most kinds of speeches.
- Always cite your sources of information.
- Use trusted sources of information that won't politicize your data or alienate your audience. Don't quote Fox News to a liberal audience, or NPR to a conservative one; don't quote a nine-year-old girl as a source of authority to a middle-aged audience; *do* quote a nine-year-old girl as an authority to an audience of nine-year-old girls.
- Contextualize data whenever possible in everyday, local terms. A 9 percent decrease in state taxes means how many additional oyster po'boys per household for the residents of Bayou des Glaises, Louisiana? An increased yield of 174,000 bushels of Montana spring wheat means how many tractor trailers loaded with bread?
- Vary your sources. Statistics and scientific studies are great, but so are vivid personal anecdotes, witness testimony, and historical records. Information must be credible, but it must also be expressive and stimulating.
- Don't let your data speak for you. Audiences are moved less by facts than by speakers' beliefs and personal conviction. Your data might be convincing, but if you're not engaged

with it, why not just email a spreadsheet? Tell your audience how you feel and why it matters.

Make Your Point with Visual Aids

Slides, charts, props, graphics, videos, and physical demonstrations convey reams of information at a glance. They also help to keep the texture of a presentation fluid and lively. Despite their usefulness, it's important to remember that your audience has come to see *you*, not your slides. Here are five rules for using visual aids effectively:

- Keep it simple. Images and slides should explain or demonstrate one idea at a time. Avoid using too many numbers, words, or visual elements on any one display.
- Limit the number of images. You're giving a speech, not showing a movie. For most kinds of presentations, you, your face, and your voice should remain the center of attention.
- Never turn your back to your audience. Just . . . seriously . . . don't. If you're not an adult entertainer, it's safe to assume that no one wants to see your backside.
- Never read from your slides. Your audience knows how to read. Remember, you're a tour guide. Your job is to explain and contextualize what they're reading, not duplicate their efforts.
- Visual aids must be varied in color and style. Expressiveness is every bit as important as logic for making your point. Stimulate your listeners' neuroreceptors in as many ways as you can.

By now, your speech should be mostly composed. You're ready to move on to the final phase of speech development.

Step 5: Practice your speech.

Find Your Voice

For Cicero, history's greatest teacher of oratory, the key to eloquence was not confidence, or intellect, or creativity, but the admittedly masochistic ability to endure the pain of preparation and rehearsal. There's no aspect of public speaking more often over-looked or short-changed than teaching your voice and body to express the speech you have—so far—diligently composed for the page.

- Begin by reading your talk aloud several times, with no attempt to be lively or smooth. Use a timer to ensure that you're within your limit. The average listener can absorb about 125 to 150 words per minute. If your speech runs long, look for ways to shorten it.

- Continue rehearsing, taking special care to enunciate clearly, listening attentively to how your words feel and sound. If they seem mushy, hollow, boring, or garbled, change them—or alter the way you're saying them. If an angry or amused tone allows you to cut extra words from your speech ("I was mad," "It was funny"), go for it.

- Record yourself or practice in front of real people, or both, if you can. This will be painful. Believe me, I understand. But it's better to hate yourself for a while *before* your speech than *during* your speech and then for every remaining moment of your life.

- Look for opportunities to vary your tone, speed, and pitch. Even "serious," data-heavy presentations are no excuse for a monotone. Does your voice correspond to what you're saying? If you're discussing something tragic, let your voice reflect it. If you're telling your audience how thrilled you are to be speaking to them, don't say it like you're facing a firing squad.

- Memorize your introduction and conclusion. Brain freeze occurs most commonly during those awful seconds when you first face a crowd. If you train yourself beforehand with this five-minute exercise, a small cluster of neurons will, almost magically, remember how to get your lips and tongue moving, despite yourself. Endings tend to bring on a similar kind of paralysis. It's all too easy to flounder at the end of your speech and taper off on a weak note ("Um, so well, *yeah!*"), leaving your bewildered audience unsure if you even finished. Commit your conclusion to memory—just a sentence or two—and it will guide you like a goalpost to the end of your speech.

Don't Forget Your Body

Your ideas and information are undoubtedly the most interesting and important part of your speech—to you. From your audience's point of view, however, the most interesting and important part of your speech is *you*—your body, the way you look, act, and seem. To be oblivious of this perspective, i.e., the fact that other people aren't you and that they don't live in your head, is to ignore the prime directive of public speaking.

To paraphrase Aristotle, when an audience finds our behavior weird or distracting, they don't believe us—even when we speak the truth. None of this means public speaking requires that you pretend to be someone you're not, but it's important to observe the following five rules to ensure that your body expresses your message instead of ruining it:

- Avoid unconscious gestures like tapping your feet or playing with your keys. Don't touch your hair or your face. Don't repeat any single gesture so often it begins to look neurotic. Wear whatever you want—as long as it doesn't distract from the purpose of your speech.

- Practice every part of your speech as if you're actually delivering it. If you can rehearse in the room or space where you'll be speaking, great. If not, improvise. Will you be approaching the lectern from a seat far away? Practice walking to the stage. Will you be asking your audience rhetorical questions? Give them as many seconds to answer as they would need in real life. The more your body knows about how it will feel to give your speech, the more freedom your brain will have to focus on the content of your speech.

- When you talk to friends and family, your body works in tandem with your words. The fish you caught was THIS big (hands stretching wide). That dude on the bus was CRAZY (finger twirling around your ear). If you stiffen up before a crowd and break off all use of your hands, body, and facial expressions as you talk, *you'll* look like the crazy person. You don't need to be an actor, but you do need to use your body to help illustrate what you're talking about, just as you do in normal conversation. Practice and perfect the gestures that will help you do so.

- Keep it moving. It's hard for an audience to enjoy your message if you're visibly petrified. Instead of standing rigidly rooted to one spot, stretch out a bit, if space allows. Occupy the stage. Take the opportunity to engage with different members and sections of the audience.
- Script your gestures, if need be. Churchill did it, Dave Chappelle does it, and so can you. In the margins of your written speech, write down when to pause, when to take a sip of water, when to move to the far side of the stage, and so on. If it sounds canned, so be it. The greatest irony of rehearsing a speech is that the more you prepare, the more natural you will be.

Conclusion

Very few of us are naturally eloquent. If it's any consolation, students in ancient times spent years studying these very techniques. I should also add that plenty of great speakers break at least some of the rules I describe above. If you rigorously embrace even half the steps in this Appendix, you'll see how and why learning to speak in public has nothing to do with overcoming shyness or changing your personality. It's a technical skill that nearly anyone can acquire. As you learn to say what you mean in the way that you mean to say it with diminishing anxiety, you'll feel what it means to represent yourself in the world honestly and ably— instead of wondering what that would be like. Good luck and be patient with yourself.

ACKNOWLEDGMENTS

As it turns out, the only thing more fraught than speaking in public is writing about it. The technical challenges of capturing the workings of live speech on the page required nearly endless experimentation over many years and commensurately infinite patience from the many friends, family, and colleagues who suffered along with the process.

The list of people whose assistance proved critical begins with my step-cousin Bill von Hunsdorf, who, I'm sad to note, passed away in 2018. His story opened my eyes to what I now feel is the biggest subject we've never noticed. After him came my friend and agent, Bill Clegg, whose many years of moral, technical, and professional support were invaluable. I'm deeply grateful to Toastmasters' executive management, especially Suzanne Frey, for trusting me early on enough to let me contact random club members. Their unvarnished testimonials about the organization proved helpful beyond measure.

I outlasted a platoon of editors at Random House, beginning with Dan Menaker, continuing with Jonathan Jao, then David Ebershoff, and culminating with Annie Chagnot, whose many long and insightful hours of collaboration will never be forgotten. I'd also like to thank an embarrassingly long list of allies, readers, and supporters, each of whom helped shape a chapter, idea, or lesson or otherwise lent assistance of myriad varieties: Sam Douglas; Mike Levine; Shauna Lyon; Clancy Nolan; Heather McGowan; Tara Bray Smith; Andrew Urtz; Sabin Streeter; Eric Konigsberg; my sister, Marisa; my mother, Sonia Bowe-Gutman; my stepmother, Lynn Bowe; Michael Valenti; Peter Spear; A. V. Flox; Ingrid Bernstein; David Warner; Mayer Rus; Darcy Cosper; and Kenneth Crab. Whatever praise and thanks I can express with this sentence falls far short of the hours of guidance, collaboration, and sustenance I received from each one of them.

Dozens of Toastmasters helped by sharing their lives and stories with me: Andy Little, from Milwaukee; Shana Iravani, from Thousand Oaks, California; Roy Chenier, Ashanti Witherspoon, and Cheryl Cayhee, from Baton Rouge, Louisiana; Al Hoffman, Margo Forster, and Gordon Andersen, from my Speakeasy meeting in Saint Louis Park, Minnesota; author Susan Cain; pizza magnate Tom Monaghan; cookie impresario Debbi Fields Rose; former NBA star Mark Eaton; and many others.

Scores of non-Toastmasters offered invaluable insights as well, including speech coach and author Joe Dolce; Anett D. Grant, president, Executive Speaking, Inc; David Lavin, president and CEO, the Lavin Agency; Eve Meyer, former executive director of San Francisco Suicide Prevention hotline; University of Houston professor of rhetoric James Kastely; Dr. Rhonda Zaharna, director of the global media program in the School of Communication, American University; Dr. Giorgio Ganis, associate professor in cognitive neuroscience, University of Plymouth School of Psychology.

To the many people whose contributions and interviews didn't make it into the book, thanks all the same. You know who you are; I will be available when my turn comes to help.

SOURCES

There are thousands of books about rhetoric, public speaking, communication, language, and related subjects like debate, acting, and vocal training, dozens of which I found helpful for understanding the lost, ancient approach to eloquence. I have tried here to include only those I found most informative, or which I mentioned most often and directly in these pages. I will steer clear of citing "hard" or social-scientific studies, which seemed less pertinent to the subject of speech training and its place in a democratic society, with the sole exception of those produced by the Pew Research Center, a nonpartisan fact tank that does an amazing job of informing the public about issues, attitudes, and trends shaping the world.

Aristotle. *Ars Rhetorica.* The translation by W. Rhys Roberts is available online: classics.mit.edu/Aristotle/rhetoric.html.
Bishop, Bill, with Robert G. Cushing. *The Big Sort: Why the Clustering of Like-minded America Is Tearing Us Apart.* Houghton Mifflin Company, 2008.

Burke, Kenneth. *A Rhetoric of Motives.* University of California Press, 1950.

Cicero, Marcus Tullius. *On the Ideal Orator.* Translated by James M. May and Jakob Wisse. Oxford University Press, 2001.

Conley, Thomas. *Rhetoric in the European Tradition.* University of Chicago Press, 1990.

Goffman, Erving. *The Presentation of Self in Everyday Life.* Anchor Books, 1959.

Kennedy, George A. *Comparative Rhetoric: An Historical and Cross-Cultural Introduction.* Oxford University Press, 1997.

———. *A New History of Classical Rhetoric.* Princeton University Press, 1994.

Leith, Sam. *Words Like Loaded Pistols: Rhetoric from Aristotle to Obama.* Basic Books, 2012.

Noonan, Peggy. *Simply Speaking: How to Communicate Your Ideas with Style, Substance, and Clarity.* ReganBooks, 1998.

Pinker, Steven. *The Stuff of Thought.* Penguin Books, 2007.

Poulakos, Takis, and David Depew, eds. *Isocrates and Civic Education.* University of Texas Press, 2004.

Putnam, Robert D. *Bowling Alone: The Collapse and Revival of American Community.* Simon & Schuster, 2000.

Rodenburg, Patsy. *The Right to Speak: Working with the Voice.* Routledge, 1992.

Sennett, Richard. *The Fall of Public Man.* Knopf, 1977.

Smedley, Ralph C. *Personally Speaking.* Toastmasters International, 1966.

ABOUT THE AUTHOR

John Bowe has contributed to *The New Yorker, The New York Times Magazine, GQ, McSweeney's, This American Life,* and many others. He is the co-editor of *Gig: Americans Talk About Their Jobs* (Crown, 1999); editor of *Us: Americans Talk About Love* (Faber USA, 2010); and author of *Nobodies: Modern American Slave Labor and the Dark Side of the New Global Economy* (Random House, 2007). He co-wrote the screenplay for the movie *Basquiat.* He is a recipient of the J. Anthony Lukas Work-in-Progress Award, the Hillman Prize, the Richard J. Margolis Award, and the Harry Chapin Media Award, for reporting on hunger- and poverty-related issues. He lives in New York City.

johnfbowe.com
Instagram: @j0hnb0we

ABOUT THE TYPE

This book was set in Bembo, a typeface based on an old-style Roman face that was used for Cardinal Pietro Bembo's tract *De Aetna* in 1495. Bembo was cut by Francesco Griffo (1450–1518) in the early sixteenth century for Italian Renaissance printer and publisher Aldus Manutius (1449–1515). The Lanston Monotype Company of Philadelphia brought the well-proportioned letterforms of Bembo to the United States in the 1930s.